MW00898642

*Supplemental*

# SKILLS OF THE ASSASSIN

## Devil's Advocacy

*Supplemental*
# SKILLS OF THE ASSASSIN
Devil's Advocacy

# R.J. GODLEWSKI

*Eliminating elitism from defense.*

*Supplemental Skills of the Assassin: Devil's Advocacy*

©2018 R.J. Godlewski

Printed by CreateSpace Independent Publishing Platform

*All Rights Reserved*

ISBN-13: 978-1519513410
ISBN-10: 1519513410

# TABLE OF CONTENTS

A LEGACY OF SKILLS                    11

A MATTER OF CONTROL                   17

INTRODUCING *EVIL*                    27

UNFATHOMABLE JUSTICE                  37

A TIME FOR A KILLING                  51

VIATICUM                             61

ABSENTE REO                          73

A LEGION OF ONE                      85

FINAL SKILLS                         97

ABOUT THE AUTHOR                     107

# DEDICATION

*To absolute freedom from Evil.*

# ACKNOWLEDGMENTS

To God the Father, the Son, and the Holy Spirit, without Whom I would find no talent, no opportunity, and no friends with which to affect either my trade or my interests.

*Deo gratias.*

And to Mother Mary, *Our* Mother, whose simple "May it be done according to your word" led to the Salvation of all humanity. Thank you!

# A LEGACY OF SKILLS

IN FULL DISCLOSURE, I had intended to write only one book on the skillset of an independent assassin, 2012's *Skills of the Assassin: Understanding the Tactics of the Professional Killer*. Published in rather colloquial speech, I did not intend for the book to reach many desks of professional security personnel, but when the book became recommended reading for several college courses, it took on a life of its own and, perhaps understandably, the wrath of many critics. These readers took exception to the book's release, covering all grievances from the style of writing on through questioning my academic background in the process. Obviously, I struck a nerve somewhere.

Two years later, in 2014, I released *More Skills of the Assassin: Delving Deeper into Human Depravity* as partial response to these criticisms. Mostly, however, I wanted to release material that I had intended to include within the first book but chose to withhold because, frankly, I did not know how well the first option would prevail. Such books could not be targeted for "best seller" lists, regardless, and therefore I strove to influence a very small audience. And I did, judging by both positive and negative criticisms. Of course, I do *not* write to receive accolades or professional endorsements. I write to tell stories and, insofar as possible, teach the reader something new that he or she may not have considered before.

Now you hold within your hands, yet *another* book on the skillsets of professional assassins and you may be wondering "*Why?*" Of what possible motive – or knowledge – tempts me to construct another book on a subject far less familiar than that, say, of neutron stars? Frankly, I write about what I *want* to write about, and little more. I author my books because I sense a need to write about certain subjects, which is why you will find my books on corporate security, personal defense, and guerrilla warfare alongside texts on religious faith and even fiction novels.

In the first *Skills* I broached the subject of the techniques of independent, professional killers in a way that may dilute the subject for broader audiences. In *More Skills*, I narrowed the focus towards select individuals who found themselves within the field and employed this foundation to build upon the notion that, despite Hollywood fascinations, just about *anyone* could emerge as a professional killer. I needn't have elaborated upon the first offering, but I did nevertheless.

I wrote both books to instigate discussion, level a charge against censorship, and, most of all, tweak the demonic mind that swirls within even the most puritan of persons. In other words, I wanted to write books that cast a devilish spin on what should be "expected" within civilized company. In a world deluged with political correctness, I simply wanted to write a couple of books that would unnerve a few of my more cultured colleagues. But that is not the *whole story*. It couldn't be.

Looking back upon the last four years, I realized that what I offered through my books came, necessarily, from a perspective that no other author could produce. That is, whomever writes, pens from the heart and the mind of a particular person and represents that person's *unique* experiences, lessons, and observations. It is as obvious as an individual athlete taking credit for their successes even though a great many others may have trained and sponsored them throughout the years. Individuality is not necessarily a team effort, but all individuals transit various 'teams' within life.

In my relatively short fifty-five years of life, I have witnessed the horrors of earthly existence, experienced death up close and personal far more times than I wish to consider, and, most importantly, found myself within the company of some rather notorious individuals whose "occupations" would sour the soul of a great many other professionals. In short, I have *lived* a life, not run away from it. Too many people today shy away from the lessons and opportunities that his or her life entails for fear of realizing that that life represents reality and not fantasy.

Oh, what lessons I could have learned had members of my family who struggled through the 1920s and 1930s street gangs of urban America been able to write down their experiences regarding that turbulent environment. Too often, today, we dismiss the industrial for the technological, the empirical for the indoctrination. Our "anything goes" social communities merely shepherd in the notion that anything contrary to our expectations must be equally shepherded out. Because of this, we fight gun violence with gun control, illegal immigration with legislation, and disease with promiscuity.

Social media, that great "leveler" of education, has descended into a great enabler of deceit, disgust, and perversion. We no longer seek knowledge for personal growth; rather, we seek information for political advantage. Which is precisely why I have elected to release a heretofore unnecessary third installment of the so-called *Skills* series. In discussing independent, professional killing, we must further eliminate the broad accusations of nonsense in order to inspect the presence of people who kill for a living. And, no, frankly, gang bangers and drug traffickers do not kill for a living. They merely kill as an opportunity for survival.

My argument rests within the first chapter of this book – people love being in *control*. We want to be in control of anything and everything, especially of those things that work against our sensibilities. Want to control the masses? Eliminate firearms. What to control industry? Enforce climate change legislation. Want to control society? Promote entertainers and musicians as worthy of emulation. Want to control your adversary? Silence them *permanently*. It remains as old as Cain and Abel.

As long as there are people who care less about money, they will pay any fee to retain control, even going as far as to order – quite retail – the killing of a competitor or adversary. This plain and straightforward, "no cure, no pay" arrangement means that there will always be individuals who would rather pay a premium to ensure that he or she retains full control over whatever grievance they perceive.

Most people raised within the Christian West subscribe, even though mostly subconsciously, to the Gospel tradition of "grinning and bearing it". In other words, to emulate Christ, again even if only subconsciously, we must love our enemies, bear our crosses, and live out our own "Passion" of enduring this horrible world for greater glory within the hereafter. Unfortunately, life – even eternal life – is not so accommodating.

For a culture that, say, turns a Levant-raised carpenter who battled demonic rule for three decades into a socially just, rather anemic revolutionary, we have lost the battle against diabolical hatred in order to shield ourselves from primal reality. Without this mental and physical toughness, we remain little more than 'wet noodles' occupying bodies forged within millions of years of survival of the fittest. Alas, when confronted with cold-blooded killings, we run off screaming "Help us!" into the night. And we expect that help to come from one of two sources.

In the first case, we openly declare that people's environments dictate his or her actions. In this regard, we can cease killing by simply providing healthcare, education, money, and "safe spaces" for the unfortunate who want to harm us. Hence, people are just products of his or her environment and as soon as we can effectively legislate that world, we can transform them into productive members of society. Within the second consideration, we merely dismiss reality in favor of fantasy.

We term, for instance, the brutal "denial of life" imparted towards the unborn as a woman's "natural right" to procure an abortion. Or, perhaps, an elderly person's "right" to end his or her life whenever *they* determine it unworthy of enduring. In short, anything industrialized becomes permissible because we merely *progress* into a more enlightened civilization devoid of those archaic notions of being responsible for one's actions.

For whatever it is worth, *this* is precisely why I have decided to author a third version of *Skills*; the world needs to come to grips with the notion of individuals so diabolical in their coldness towards life and death, that they can drive your kids to Sunday school on the weekends and yet rip out your tongue or slit your chest open for whatever salary matches his or her expectation. People that can dissect another living soul with as much precision and grace as a skilled surgeon and yet walk amongst us without drawing even a casual glance. Someone that can spread absolute terror into the minds of the most inhuman tyrant and, yet, gracefully present their art collection to the world.

Prepare to meet the most diabolical creature imaginable...


R.J. Godlewski
October 2018
Iowa

# A MATTER OF CONTROL

CONTROL REPRESENTS THE very lifeblood of tyranny. If we cannot accept a particular condition, then we simply try to eliminate that posing problem. In the Biblical book of Genesis, the serpent knew that he could not 'kill' an omnipresent God, so he decided to taint the most precious of creatures: Man. He did so through the implementation of sin and doubt as to a person's absolute reliance upon his or her Creator for all necessary things. His declaration that, "You will certainly not die! No, God knows well that the moment you eat of [the tree of life] your eyes will be opened and you will be like gods who know what is good and what is bad" (Genesis 3:4-5 *New American Bible*). In the tale, people sinned through this desire of controlling his or her own lives and the devil worshipped the idea that sin enabled him and his legions to control this control.

Even from amongst the non-religious, this mastery of control cannot be overstated. Whatever crime, whatever agenda, whatever vice represents a manifestation of *control*. Burglary suggests a control of money. Pornography suggests a control of sexual desire. Legislation suggests a control of the population. Militaries suggest a control of adversaries. Religion suggests a control of the soul. And, yes, killing suggests a control of others' lives. If you have it, you want to control it. If you need it, then someone *else* holds control over it.

To eliminate this control from another bearer, there remain only three possible options. You can negotiate for it, ignore it, or take it back by force. In the first case, for example, few people bear an interest within the labors of baking a loaf of bread, so they drive to their local grocery and select (negotiate) a product that meets his or her needs and price. For the second, a middle-income family might find the need for a new automobile, but a strict budget may prevent them from acquiring the vehicle at that particular time, so they essentially ignore the sales pitches of dealers (or even friends) despite the latter holding what might be important for that family's wellbeing. In the last example, a criminal temporarily holds control over their victim, but that victim may ultimately decide to fight back in order to restore control over his or her own safety and survival.

Criminals, unfortunately, usually do not negotiate – in the manner that most of us refer to the term – nor do they wish to ignore opportunities *unless it means surrendering their own control* over matters. In view of this, if he or she does *not* hold control over the situation, they generally take it by force. The illegal drug trade is representative of this; most trafficking organizations violently fight for *control* of lucrative routes, landing strips, and customers.

Control, obviously, is not always a good thing, for as with almost every endeavor, "too much" can lead to obsession. People literally tend to "lose control" of themselves whenever they try to remain too in control of his or her actions. In fact, the etymology associated with the word *insane* derives from the loss in control of one's mental state. Yet, being "insane" does not imply that one bears the capacity to formulate a strategy of murder and carry out that order with the fullest intention of escaping apprehension.

Most people – even those with a preference for being in absolute control – do not transgress into innate criminality. No, that condition warrants continual outside influence. Here is where we divert from the purely human and involve ourselves into the diabolic. From the partly physical and partly spiritual into the absolute spiritual. From the lackadaisical approach of most human individuals into the eternally "on" mechanism of the demonic world.

Murder, as with most crimes, occurs via one of two thought processes: spontaneous or calculated. One either seizes upon an opportunity or they develop into a definite mindset. Sometimes, even, an individual encroaches upon both scenarios – such as when a seasoned pickpocket notices a distracted shopper's handbag – but mostly we can restrict criminality to either persuasion.

Regarding murder, those who engage within the spontaneous variety often nurture a lingering ability to commit the act. For example, a well-mannered father may repeatedly beat the rapist of his young daughter until the former dies. Such an event may be somewhat drastic, but the love of the individual's daughter bore a subliminal desire to protect her at all costs – even to the point of killing an attacker. This reaction is caused by simple *hate* – the sinister sibling of love.

When we move away from spontaneous murder into its more premeditated variety, we equally distance ourselves from the raw emotions of 'hated' into indifference – the *true* opposite of love. Here is where we find the cold, calculating individual that can murder at the proverbial drop of a hat. These individuals are not motivated by opportunity; they fashion that opportunity to kill. Why?

Many psychiatrists have explored the concept of the diabolical from the psychological angle and there exists no true consensus regarding the matter. Some people just seem *born to kill*. To analyze them, we must, again, consider the decidedly unpopular notion of Evil (in the form of creatures whose passion remains to destroy the grace of human lives). In order not to confuse the nonreligious, however, we shall dispense with theology and discuss the matter from the synopsis.

Imagine, if you will, a creature whose actions are not tainted by a physical body. They grow neither tired nor hungry, nor do they age. They travel at the speed of thought and forget nothing. Now imagine that such a creature bears sufficient knowledge of any human individual that they encounter. They intimately understand that person's desires, fears, anxieties, and physical limitations. Finally, these creatures bear an unfathomable desire to destroy human civilization, one soul at a time. Might not such a creature seek out and choose vulnerable individuals to *control?* What might their prime action be?

If we take such considerations at face value, we can begin to understand how some individuals seem to swirl within matters of violent criminal activity. For example, we *could* begin to understand the absolute violence and intimidation inherent within gangs such as the notorious MS-13. They kill, maim, and dehumanize their subjects without ceasing. Yet, there is a certain passion – or hatred – within his or her actions that speaks of the duality of love. In this regard, we must, of course, consider the Darwinian law of ferocity increasing within two similar species. That is, street gangs need to remain in control of their territory, so they engage within violence to defeat similar groups whether they are rival gangs, law enforcement, or other civil leaders.

From the broader perspective, organized groups such as MS-13 remain *human* – albeit from a primal perspective. Others, however, kill from strict indifference; they carry no emotions whether from love or hatred. These individuals can kill a stranger as if simply punching in with the timeclock at work. They murder without either hatred or anger and never regret his or her actions. Their sanitized crime is what makes them so feared by normal human beings, for we always seem to impart some measure of psychological disorder upon those who view human lives as mere commodities.

Because people need to be in control, we automatically define those who disagree with our viewpoint as "out of control" and this merely exacerbates the situation. That is, *we* may be the ones experiencing control issues because those who kill for career remain very regulated indeed. They spend weeks, if not months, planning the perfect crime and will only accept a contract if it meets their conditions for survival. Most citizens, to the contrary, struggle to survive paycheck to paycheck.

To understand professional killers (as distinguished

from the openly psychotic), we *must delve more deeply into understanding this concept of control.* To do this effectively, we must shed our present notions of precisely what "control" represents and view the subject from both external and internal considerations. In our discussion, this turns to two perspectives: the control of the murderer's mind and the criminal's control of his or her function. Both are distinct and yet interconnected.

To commit murder repetitively, one must not engage within the practice indiscriminately, for to do so suggests spontaneity and, henceforth, lack of direction. While it may seem somewhat fanciful to view any wanton killer as having discretion, we must understand that we are discussing professional, *paid* killers here and not the subordinate variety that follows the group absolution dynamics of street gangs. In this regard, the subject matter rests with the individual that will only accept contracts in which he or she is guaranteed both a profit *and* an opportunity to escape from connection with the crime for the duration. Yet, we are *further* discussing the mindset of the killer's client.

The process of "ordering" a killing requires the same level of emotional distance from the act as does the crime itself, but here is where the client deviates a bit from the proprietor. The client controls the assassin's mind from the perspective that he or she must persuade the killer to accept the mission at hand, itself involving more of a percentage of the assassin's career than, say, the services of an attorney or architect would require. In this regard, the client must offer both sufficient reason and money to affect the interest of the killer.

This control, partially realistic and partially supportive, is what drive's the contractor to accept the assignment. In other words, he or she must consider the following:

✓ What obstacles prevent me from reaching my target?
✓ How much time will it take me just to realize a

possible outcome?
- ✓ What resources must I have in place to retreat from culpability for the mission?
- ✓ How will this particular effort affect subsequent missions?

So how does a client "control" these considerations? In the first part, the client illustrates a strong sense of professionalism in his or her approach to the assassin. This, more than anything else, inspires the hunter to seek out the prey. This can be said because most professional killers like to project a sense of operational superiority themselves; the trade representing more of an art than a science. It represents the basic human element of "I am *damn good* at what I do!" Furthermore, it shows that the client has fully considered the implications of their action; that the targeted killing is not simply because of hatred, resentment, or chance.

Think about this for a moment. A client ordering a murder must present him or herself as a rational, respectful human being – things that we do not normally associate with killing members of the human species. Yet, this is precisely what the professional killer is looking for; a chance to affect broader change within the world, for good or bad.

Now, we must turn to discussions of a more psychological and spiritual nature regarding the control of both the assassin's and his or her client's mind. Here is where we turn from the objective towards the subjective and consider what is not normally discussed in polite company. To engage within premeditated murder – perhaps the lengthiest premeditation within such crimes – does require an absolute disconnect from viewing human beings as anything other than mere commodities.

For instance, an arsonist may burn down a building because he is fascinated with fire. Or, perhaps, a thief engages within stealing because he or she bears a gambling addiction and needs the money. Professional assassins – and the parties that employ them – do not bear such "understandable" traits. They simply view human life with the same indifference that the blind view a sunset or the deaf the cry of a small child. They see individual lives as mere mechanisms of the higher order, and that "higher order" represents the effects that the procured assassination offers.

Again, we are not discussing street violence here where murders happen by way of territorial control; these murders of the more professional variety are designed to appear as if *anything* but murder. Frankly, only diabolical Evil can affect a person in such a way because even raw hatred remains a fleeing emotion (and emotions represent passion, a decidedly noticeable attribute). And herein, once again, we must divert from Hollywood rubbish.

Evil is not affected by a demonic being with horns, a flashy red suit, and emerges from within a storm of flames. No, those are decidedly religious aspects designed to foster resentment of the beast. In reality, Evil represents a spiritual intelligence that can only affect natural laws and tempt human free will. In this regard, the "enemy" is unseen, superior in intelligence, and extremely deceptive in nature – basically the same attributes of any military or foreign foe known to nations.

What we must focus on, however, remains the *control* that such a creature can inflict upon other creatures, even if we must continue discussing the issue from a decidedly religious angle. With greater intellect, a being becomes less adaptive in nature. For example, whenever we consider a "genius", such as Mozart or Einstein, for instance, we necessarily focus upon a fundamental set of rules – both music and physics are limited by a known set of laws, even if we merely discover them at a later date. In the former case, Mozart's talent has thrilled audiences for centuries, but music in and of itself bears only seven natural notes from which to work with.

In regard to the natural world – Einstein's environment – no matter how extraordinary new revelations appear, physics still must dwell upon the laws through which our physical universe plays out. In other words, there is *no unnatural way* in which our sun can explode as a supernova (answer: it takes a *lot* more mass – and there are perfectly *natural* ways in which this could be conceived). The same remains with music, whether you enjoy classical Beethoven or the J. Geils Band, you still must build your repertoire on those seven natural notes and their various keys.

When the discussion turns towards controlling the human mind, we can forego such thoughts as hexes, voodoo, and curses. There remains a very *natural* way in which the seemingly "supernatural" can control our thoughts and actions and we have already discussed these. An evil creature can plant thoughts and suggestions into our minds through the recollection of memories, anxieties, fears, and desires amongst other psychological images. Because of our free will, we *cannot* do anything that we do not want to do; the only way for us to bypass this will is to freely offer it up ourselves. And this is where heretofore 'decent people' conduct the most horrendous actions, be it, say, thievery, adultery, or murder.

The *only way* that an individual can override his or her basic subconscious intention is for "someone else" to make it appear more appealing, more profitable, or more desirous. In our case, the procuring of professional death of the manner in which we are discussing requires the removal of *all emotional thoughts* normally associated with human activities. Here is where Evil exists; emotionless murder can only come by way of extinguishing the regret factor inherent within the human species (e.g., both Adam and Eve and their son, Cain, ultimately regretted their sins – to draw upon an ancient Biblical example).

Professional assassins and their clients are *not* emotional people, for either would simply choose a more practical option such as shooting their prey in the head. After all, dead is dead. Where they divert, however, rests with the strongest intention of denying disclosure of the crime to the broader world. And this takes an extraordinary level of diabolical control to carry out. Something that mere *humans* are not inherently capable of.

The prospect of possessing bodies – even the extraordinary physique of special operations soldiers, say – means that the normal human mind is confronted with fatigue, hunger, injuries, and such other things that keep people from truly functioning within a 24/7 capacity. Nevertheless, as one finds upon viewing the television news for even the briefest of moments, Evil remains ceaseless. Yet, 'it' understands that even gang bangers sleep; sooner or later, even the most notorious 'Public Enemy' finds need for a rest. Because of this, professional killers are not sprinters; they remain marathon runners within their trade.

When emotion leads to disaster, killers must remain even-keeled, without the slightest perturbation defeating what may have required months to plan out. The slightest emotion, whether anger, jealousy, envy, greed, etc., that heralds ordinary killing, will doom the professional. For this reason, anyone desiring to control the mind of either an assassin or his or her client must engage within rather sanitary thought manipulation. That is, one must be controlled discreetly or else he or she may fight off the suggestion – which is why "hearts and minds" campaigns generally fail for militaries.

Desensitization remains the key for influencing individuals normally constrained under expectations of sin, taboo, or incarceration. It is also a strong deceptive measure, for the surest way to desensitize someone is to get him or her to disbelieve that they are, in fact, being desensitized. For example, we get teenagers to play violent videogames for "enjoyment" when, regardless of your personal beliefs, there remains no true enjoyment in harming another person (the deception being that we are "only playing a game"). Under the auspices of playing "games", a person can reliably state that they are *not* harming anyone because it is thus merely a game – though we are still playing out a fantasy of harming individuals through the group absolution of online gamers and software manufacturers.

That this control is deceptive cannot go without notice, but it takes a rational mind to forestall accusations of one becoming too preachy. That is, Hollywood production companies, for instance, routinely spread the concept of violence and employing firearms for effect when, in public, they often depict gun ownership as villainous. Their intention is duplicitous. First, they control the thought that violence remains entertainment. Second, they employ controlling behavior to suggest that "everyone else" is at fault.

In the discussion of professional killers, we can see this reality unfold in several directions. Killing becomes a normal way of life, its impact upon the practitioner remains negligible, and its provision as a service little more than a chosen option amongst someone *else*. Here we dismiss the sin, excuse the sinner, and, when all else fails, corrupt the masses. These subjects will be covered in more detail throughout this book, but, for now, we simply need to engage the primal concept of being in *control.*

The assassination in question bears three fundamental elements of such control:

1. The client ascertains a need to control his or her situation and believes that the killing of an adversary represents the ultimate way to silence the opposition;

2. The assassin specializes in controlling other's lives to the point where he or she can fashion the target's demise and literally get away with the murder;

3. The assassination act itself industrializes the control of all parties – the target is dead, and both provider and procurer remain tightly locked within one another through knowledge of each other's participation.

Again, the ultimate tyranny represents complete control over another's life and death is, more than anything else, effectively *permanent.* So, now, just *why* is that death so important?

# INTRODUCING *EVIL*

IT CAN BE fathomed that most people within the world remain either abhorred at death or view it as a matter of fact way of life. In this regard, very few consider the actual employment of death as a panacea for any particular problem, let alone one that they wish to pay for and accept accountability, no matter how clandestinely, perhaps for the remainder of his or her life. To understand 'death for hire', we must always step back into historical time and gauge human actions from the primordial. And here is where we bring *religion* into review, if only because the subject retains the antiquity of human evolutionary thought.

Everything within the physical world was created; brought forth from some progenitor. From the purely scientific perspective, for example, massive supergiant stars explode into supernovae showering the cosmos with heavy elements, many of which make up our own human bodies – not to mention the oxygen that we need to breathe. In monotheistic religion, the issue at hand becomes not *how* carbon and oxygen from exploding stars ended up within our blood, but precisely *why*. Specifically, Jews, Christians, and Muslims believe that an Omnipotent God, serving as Creator, ushered everything into existence (through His choice of mechanisms and timing). Understandably, this latter view dismisses the *physical* for the *spiritual*.

Unfortunately, many nonadherent individuals – or, at least, agnostics – wrongly view the spiritual as either unnatural or, perhaps, even, supernatural, never accepting the notion that spirits may, indeed, belong to the natural world. Hollywood movies and fantasy novels remain much to blame for this divergent from the natural into the supernatural, but for monotheists the physical world remains but an extension of the spiritual, representing both its apex and its cause. Our lives, on earth, represent a brief interlude between our spiritual perfection and our present tainted nature – which brings us to the concept of just how humans became so tainted and imperfect in the first place.

To understand this intrinsic nature between people and evil, we must retreat to the story offered by Christianity – specifically Roman Catholicism – and provide the narrative shared by a large percentage of people throughout history. For our purposes, however, we shall refrain from undue theology and present the case study as succinctly as possible to illustrate our discussion about such evil:

In the beginning, to coin the Biblical phrase, God created the universe and His spiritual companions to serve and worship their Creator. This universe served the basis for a Master Plan, the creation of a human population that entailed both a spiritual element (the soul) as well as a physical nature (the body). More importantly, God would ultimately fuse with his earthly creatures and become one of them (God being all-powerful, He could do whatever He wanted), thus elevating human nature above even the lofty "angels", the proper name given to spirits inhabiting a particular "office" within the spiritual kingdom.

As beings with great intellect but even greater free will, a large number of these spirits rebelled against God and His Plan for the universe. Their immense pride caused them to hate the 'human plan' and fight against obedience towards God. Key amongst these rebellious spirits, was their greatest intellect, Lucifer, arguably from the choir of Cherubim, whose stature in Heaven rested just below the Seraphim whose task remained to surround their Lord with praise unceasingly. After an intense battle with archangel Saint Michael, Lucifer (known also by the name of Satan – Hebrew for God's adversary or accuser – or the Devil – from the Greek word *Diabolos*) and his minions from lower angelic choirs were cast out from Heaven and forced to dwell within the natural world. Due to their intense hatred of *everything* created by God and, especially, human beings, their function turned towards tempting people into sin through disobedience towards God's Will. That God would ultimately still arrive on earth, as fully human and yet fully God, to die for our sins merely exacerbated the hatred of the Devil and his demons because *they,* being only spirits, could *not* be offered salvation once they had turned against God.

In these few brief paragraphs, we can detect the sinister threat against humans. When we consider that, as implied within St. Thomas Aquinas's *Summa Theologica*, that the myriad of spirits in the world remain as different from one another as people are from elephants, coupled with their unceasing energy, ability to affect *natural* physical laws, and knowledge of our innermost fears, desires, and memories, we can perceive a radical threat against human free will. It is, therefore, little wonder that that which routinely ails the human species is often attributed to the supernatural or unexplained psychoses.

Now, returning to our discussion of assassins and their influence over people, we can detect elements of both control *and* Evil within the course of history. That is, we can see how his or her function serves little but to dehumanize their subject to the point where raw hatred – a decidedly *creature* characteristic – gives way to the diabolical indifference offered to their intended victims. When, as discussed within the first *Skills of the Assassin*, he or she spends weeks and months getting to know their victims on a level of intimacy that very few spouses can match, the astute researcher must consider the presence of a superior intellect (if so diabolical) at work.

Street gangs, Mafiosi, and Islamic jihadists *all* introduce emotion into their violence granting their victims, if little else, a sincere degree of appreciation. This is most emphatically *not* the case with independent assassinations, most of which occur in the world with relatively little notice by the public. Even the most stoical individual must appreciate this sense of disconnect from the broader population. And, arguably, the presence of the infamous Evil spirit that exists solely to cause great harm to we human creatures. Yet, we do *not* so accord ourselves the attention towards the *unseen* that we should; it being a matter of human (dare we say, evil-induced) pride that we must suspect anything that we cannot observe firsthand.

To kill without remorse lends to considerations of deeply held psychotic disturbances. To plan, train, and conduct such murders for *specific* fees heralds a great deal more scrutiny. Mass murderers do not necessarily train, and serial killers may not always plan. Assassins bring both to a level of professionalism rare even within engineering offices. And empowering this capacity remains a very *unhumanlike* "computer".

Evil remains strictly 'digital'; an act or thought is evil, or it is not. Political or social semantics cannot change the equation. We can argue forever regarding whether particular actions are worthy or not, but, remember, *evil* remains an affront towards God and, therefore, must be viewed in context of established religious precedence (no national law permits wanton murder – even within tyrannies). Privately procured assassinations dispense with *all* established laws regardless of whether they are religious or secular in nature, for to kill for profit allows the provider to establish the rules.

Herein is where we come to the inherent evil within assassination – the *killer becomes a substitute for God*, determining who shall live and who shall die by virtue of whether he or she accepts a contract or not. Governments, for their role, tend to view the assassination business as part of religion solely to justify their participation. For instance, Israel ushers in an "eye for an eye" and Islamic nations offer to avenge sacrilege against Muhammad or Allah. Not so with the independent, contract killer.

In accepting an assignment – which is necessarily

done under a 'no cure, no pay' arrangement wherein the assassin receives no pay until *after* the target has been killed – the contractor has essentially elected to end the life of another person with whom he or she has had *zero acquaintance* heretofore. More importantly, unlike government assassins or soldiers, they have relinquished any right to blame someone else for that responsibility. A covert (more than simply clandestine) operative elects to take on a contract that, when completed, ends with the eternal silencing of another human being.

This, more than anything else, permits us to continue our discussion of "Evil" rather than another socially acceptable agent for the actions of an independent, professional killer, for there is no other malady that so affects members of the human species.

| **Expanded Homicide Data** Murder Victims by Weapon, 2010–2014 | | | | | |
|---|---|---|---|---|---|
| Weapons | 2010 | 2011 | 2012 | 2013 | 2014 |
| **Total** | **13,164** | **12,795** | **12,888** | **12,253** | **11,961** |
| Total firearms: | 8,874 | 8,653 | 8,897 | 8,454 | 8,124 |
| Handguns | 6,115 | 6,251 | 6,404 | 5,782 | 5,562 |
| Rifles | 367 | 332 | 298 | 285 | 248 |
| Shotguns | 366 | 362 | 310 | 308 | 262 |
| Other guns | 93 | 97 | 116 | 123 | 93 |
| Firearms, type not stated | 1,933 | 1,611 | 1,769 | 1,956 | 1,959 |
| Knives or cutting instruments | 1,732 | 1,716 | 1,604 | 1,490 | 1,567 |
| Blunt objects (clubs, hammers, etc.) | 549 | 502 | 522 | 428 | 435 |
| Personal weapons (hands, fists, feet, etc.)[1] | 769 | 751 | 707 | 687 | 660 |
| Poison | 11 | 5 | 13 | 11 | 7 |
| Explosives | 4 | 6 | 8 | 2 | 6 |
| Fire | 78 | 76 | 87 | 94 | 71 |
| Narcotics | 45 | 33 | 38 | 53 | 62 |
| Drowning | 10 | 15 | 14 | 4 | 14 |
| Strangulation | 122 | 88 | 90 | 85 | 89 |
| Asphyxiation | 98 | 92 | 106 | 95 | 96 |
| Other weapons or weapons not stated | 872 | 858 | 802 | 850 | 830 |

[1] Pushed is included in personal weapons.

Figure 1. FBI Statistics on Murder Weapons (U.S.)

In Figure 1, we can witness the choice of "weapons" amongst murders within the United States during 2010-2014 as compiled by the Federal Bureau of Investigation.[1] From these numbers, we can observe that there remain more than sixteen different types of "weapons" typically used within murder, suggesting at the minimum that it matters little *what* killers use to advance their art; they will employ some method for success.

Removing the articles of spontaneity and passion from the realm, we *must* consider that murder comes from a source outside that particular individual. In other words, for a *single person* to, perhaps, employ a significant number of these available weapons (not to mention, improvising others) to affect his or her trade transcends the commonality of "ordinary" murderers. Such an individual is *driven* to kill and will make use of *any* available technique, tool, or opportunity to affect the target's demise.

More to the point, we must consider how many of these FBI-tabulated weapons of choice will undoubtedly leave forensic evidence behind following their use. Only the last three *identified* categories are most used by professional assassins – drowning and asphyxiation absorbing elements of accidental deaths and strangulation by way of monofilament fishing line offering little evidence once the 'weapon' is properly melted and disposed of. Only Hollywood and government agencies employ the methods of explosives and poisons to affect their crimes.

What, then, can be *the* motivating factor to continuously invent *new* (and possibly heretofore untried – though assassins are, by nature, adept at experimentation and execution) methods of killing? Again, we must succumb to the concept of Evil. Normal human behavior does not permit people to spend years, if not decades, experimenting with death provision when he or she remains unlikely to commit, say, five or ten deaths within a lifetime. Such

---

[1] https://ucr.fbi.gov/crime-in-the-u.s/2012/crime-in-the-u.s.-2012/offenses-known-to-law-enforcement/expanded-homicide/expanded_homicide_data_table_8_murder_victims_by_weapon_2008-2012.xls. Accessed May 2018.

considerations warrant the very concept of Evil as a spiritual opponent – an extraordinarily intelligent creature with a near unlimited supply of knowledge about *individual* humans and their entire race with a ceaseless energy and no physical body to hamper its movement from through sheer thought.

Consider the implications of this again, please. Imagine if you possessed four things of near *unlimited* scope:

1. Knowledge of the human mind and all individual persons' desires, hopes, memories, fears, and addictions;
2. Unceasing energy with the ability to move at the speed of thought along with intuitive knowledge of how to manipulate nature;
3. Command of legions of comparable, if uniquely individualistic creatures;
4. *Absolute hatred* of both God and humans.

Could you *not* affect some horrible malice upon the planet? Before we continue, we must consider that, within the modern world, there is *no location* on earth that has *not been touched* by the beliefs of Western Christian thought. None. Even modern adherents of the Islamic faith profess subconsciously more to Christian patterns of action than were expressed by their faith's founder, Muhammad.

We now begin to see our world not as of a predominately physical nature subject to the mastery of humanity, but of a symbiotic duplicity between the spiritual and the physical with the latter destined to share in *both* realms after leaving this temporal earth of ours and the former lording over us in matters of intelligence, ability, and knowledge. We are, therefore, subject to a range of conflictions that tug against our sensibilities.

In the gravest sense, we are *not* masters of our own destiny; not by a long shot. Modern culture dictates that we engage within horrendous sins of self-deification: we can do as we please; we are only concerned about ourselves; and there are no others greater than us. Despite this path, however, we eventually struggle against the realization that doing as we please collides with others' desires, concern for selves still necessitates the use of others for our benefit, and, in a world of billions, others maintain talents, opportunities, and assets beyond our capabilities. In short, being human remains humbling; the more we ascribe superiority to our condition, the more likely we become inferior in production.

For most, this reality unnerves little. We go about our business and assume that what *we* bear is sufficient, albeit with the eternally present "more" to whet our ambitions. This is not the case with a select few; the presence of others' bearing more opportunities, more talents, and more of anything of desire leads them towards resentment, jealousy, envy, and, ultimately, malice. The root of this maddening effort to pursue remains, of course, *happiness*. However one defines the method, the end remains that people simply want to find happiness, whether this consists of a better job, a stronger business, a deeper relationship, or simply season tickets to the Detroit Tigers.

Regardless, people remain inherently incapable of discovering lasting happiness through temporal means. People get fired from his or her place of employment, businesses fail, soulmates die, and, well, the Detroit baseball franchise has only won two World Series championships in half a century. The point is, people direct their lives towards goals that ultimately fail to satisfy his or her subconscious needs. Here, is where we often find evil lurking; when we cannot meet our deepest desires, we often grab at them through deceit, deception, thievery, or illicit association. For assassins and their clients, it remains this latter action that necessitates the business.

Unlike, perhaps, other forms of murder, the procuring of a privately ordered assassination is not meant to intimidate in the manner of, say, *La Familia* cartel members rolling severed human heads across a crowded dance floor. Such actions bespeak of emotion and, once again, emotion leads to the ruin of a perfectly executed murder. Were the target the leader of a nation or an opposition candidate, for example, then raw emotion would generate ancillary effects of division, terror, and uncertainty. Such, of course, would not require the clandestine professional as "capturing" (or killing) the perpetrator would simply fuel these subordinate occurrences.

The primary reason that clients order assassinations bears much to do with his or her concept of the 'happiness' of which we just discussed. Killing their adversary – in the mind of the client – should provide an occasion for happiness in that whatever grievance is implied would be forever altered by the killing of the offending individual. The operative word here, although, is *should*. Whatever the target did to warrant his death could *still* be offered by another individual.

Navigating the human intellect like a wayward rudder of a ship remains the aforementioned evil presence. Some theologians like to teach on the 'before' and 'after' comparisons of Christian discipleship versus satanic evil. In their discussion, they remind their flocks that while, say, Christ adamantly ordered people *not* to sin, He was there quickly offering forgiveness to those who had strayed from the path. Conversely, these ministers acknowledge, the devil lures people into expectations of happiness and pleasure only to leave their prey abandoned once the act was committed.

People who order assassinations, for their role, similarly, often remain tempted with the notion that to kill his or her opponent would simply extinguish the underlying obstacle – and assassins understand this peculiarity of the human condition. The contract killer, too, motivated by this subliminal desire to affect things permanently, understands that his or her actions remain temporary at best, which further explains why they have chosen the field for a career. For them, it matters little whether their killing of an individual remains worthwhile in the eyes of their client; rather, they proceed on the notion that his or her function remains little more than a job that "someone" must engage within.

Without getting too religious, we now may observe

how such 'evil' manifests itself within the thought processes of both contractors and clients. Both remain focused towards a common – if not objective – goal: life manipulation via the taking of a life. The trading of one person's future for the future of another. Killing, as a panacea for wellbeing.

# UNFATHOMABLE JUSTICE

EVERY HUMAN ENDEAVOR can be summed up as either an act of life or an act of death. Despite the enormity of human diversity and thought, whatever one person does is, quite frankly, undertaken through a desire to live or a fear of dying. We play the mega millions lottery, for example, not because we are afraid of dying, but that we desire to live extraordinary. Conversely, we refrain from drinking and driving because we are afraid of dying horribly. That many may seek money in order to leave their children some inheritance when dying or others may fear living fully incapacitated does not diminish the underlying reality.

Even the most mediocre of personalities dwells upon thoughts of either barely living or dying unexpectedly. These considerations are fully human; very few consider themselves sufficiently deified or unquestionably confident. Into this realm of human normality, we inject two subconscious extremes: that of the professional assassin; and his or her client.

The procurer of assassination, by definition, remains an individual whose concept of his or her own life remains so powerful that they believe that such a life can only be shored by the death of a particular individual. Think about this for a moment. For an individual to kill (directly or indirectly) without the direct threat of being killed themselves, remains a gross violation of justifiable homicide. The client bears absolutely no fear of imminent demise and, yet, he or she orchestrates their adversary's death through the coolness and cunning of a master murderer. Why? *Something* about the target simply does not fit into the world of the client.

Whether that subject remains a threat against

business, a desire for revenge, or even the paranoid thoughts that they *may*, at some point, remain a direct threat against the client, nothing expressed exhibits a bona fide opposition towards the client's life. And yet, they have ordered that individual's death for the sole reason that the client has determined that such a person cannot be permitted to live. In a very real sense, the client has morphed into the "creator" of his or her own universe and, accordingly, merits the self-perceived right to decide *who* lives within that unique world of theirs.

As for the assassin, his or her world is not of their own creation. They remain far too indifferent towards humanity to really care who lives or dies beyond those unlikely individuals who form the basis for his or her paycheck. If they permitted personal thoughts into the equation, then they remain likely to fail at a business where indifference remains key. The professional's selection of contracts to accept or not rests firmly upon matters of success and his or her own getaway with the crime. In this environment, their "world" is not one of his or her own choosing; they simply represent tools in which *others* – clients – determine the perceived outcome.

What the professional assassin offers, to the contrary, remains extreme *confidence*. That is, *only they* can achieve the unthinkable and this is precisely why the client must choose them over any competitors (such as there is). Professionals do not play God, they simply carry out solutions with engineering proficiency. The role of deity is not the mechanism involved, but the intelligence behind the decision making. For example, a bicyclist struck by lightning as he peddles down the road is killed by a discharge of electrical energy, but the timing of his path and the occurrence of the "freak" electricity rests within God's hands.

Given this reality, we can blame the assassin for the kill, but he or she would have *no* opportunity to affect his or her trade without a client bearing the mindset that *they* can call the shots when considering another's death. In this manner, they remain far more "inhuman" than the ones who kill out of rage or hatred. For more discussion on this topic, let us consider the case of Nazi henchman Adolf Eichmann, perhaps the most notorious individual to arise from the Second World War.

*Obersturmbannführer* Eichmann was the individual directly in charge of transporting Jews east into the concentration camps of the Third Reich.[2] Directly complicit in the deaths of millions of Jews, Eichmann went to his death vehemently stating that he was merely "following orders". When Eichmann was finally located and abducted in Argentina, many of his Israeli Mossad captors find that they could not stand being in the same room as him. Not that he bore a villainous presence or image, but for the complete opposite: they could not imagine that someone that looked as if, say, a diminutive postal clerk could have orchestrated the deaths of millions of innocent people. That they found the once-mighty Nazi living in abject squalor only magnified the incredulous nature of his presence.

Here we possess concrete manifestation of evil. A meek and otherwise timid individual when, in the company of group absolution and, obviously, a superior intellectual force, engaged within the most diabolical actions ever within human history and for which he uttered not one semblance of regret. In this regard, we can argue that Eichmann bore no fantastical psychological abnormalities or physiological disturbances. His presence, prior to and following the existence of the Third Reich, offers nothing to extract him from the rest of the human population.

We have to assume, therefore, that the collective presence of the Nazi regime turned an otherwise meek and complacent individual into history's most notorious murderer (even if only primarily from the organizational point of view). This fits into our previous discussion of evil not necessarily

---

[2] For an extraordinary account of Adolf Eichmann's actions and the search and capture of the Nazi, see Bascomb, Neal, *Hunting Eichmann* (New York: Mariner Books, 2009).

representing a grotesque caricature seemingly from a cartoon episode. Evil, as pure spirit offers no appearance beyond its actions and influences upon people.

To equate the client of an assassin with the likes of an Adolf Eichmann seriously dilutes the notoriety of the latter, but in this regard the nature of killing remains the same whether the incident involves one person or an entire nation. People are merely a conduit for his or her actions, albeit a device with absolute free will. They are, as discussed within the first *Skills of the Assassin*, impacted by a sea of influences, both cyclic and linear. Each person remains assailed with a lifetime of friendships, associations, anxieties, desires, heroes, education, faiths, in beyond the requisites of culture, heritage, and maturity.

These influences, however, are retained for effect by evil spirits under the leadership of Satan (or simple environmental disturbances for those not religiously inclined). They assault the human mind until the individual retreats into his or her will or abdicates and carries out the temptation. We could almost hear these influences being imparted upon Adolf Eichmann: "These people are merely *Jews...*", "You are only *sending* them away...", "It is Nazi *leadership* that holds responsibility, *not* your conscience..." and so forth.  For the rest of humanity, these tempting thoughts would appear rather desperate and criminal, but for someone predisposed to, perhaps, elevating his ego above the concern for others and, well, you bear an Adolf Eichmann.

Influencing *assassins*, to the contrary, remains a bit different for one cannot truly influence those minds that herald a cold, calculating personality. Emotions such as hatred, envy, and, of course, *power* do not translate well for longevity (despots rarely endure). Any individual adept at planning an assassination for months is most emphatically not an individual susceptible to mental temptations. Nor are they likely to be driven into irrationality.

In this regard, Evil's influence upon professional killers remains less about *suggestions* than about *extractions*;

when you cannot entice, you simply distance. It is easier, therefore, to refrain from considering murder as the intentional act of killing an innocent human being than it is a matter of cold statistics; people representing little more than bodies walking around ignorant of the broader world.

The reader may not quite understand this total indifference to human beings, but there exists a perennial social example: abortion. Regardless of one's political views, abortion represents the intentional ceasing of an infant's life through mechanical or chemical means. A fetus, in reality, is neither an organ nor is it mere tissue; it represents a ripening human individual complete with its own DNA, eye color, hair color, and experiences (yes, babies *can* hear, see, and *learn* while in the womb). Left to its own devices, a fetus *cannot* turn into an ostrich anymore than it can become a leg.

As a *complete* human being (physical deformities notwithstanding, because humans are not bound to bear two legs, two eyes, etc. for them to be *human*), the infant within the womb remains a human individual. Being "born" has little determination upon that soul's condition within the human race.[3] Regardless, by many estimates, there are roughly 45 *million* abortions conducted throughout the world every year and approximately that many within the United States alone since abortion became the law of the land in 1973. That represents more individuals denied humanity than occurred within Nazi Germany or Soviet Russia. Why?

Proponents of abortion shower their critics with statements running the gamut from being a "woman's right" on through "medical necessity". If, however, women bear fundamental rights, then such rights begin within the womb. On the other hand, if there remains a medical necessity where a human life (in its most innocent environment) needs

---

[3] Worth noting, the author's late wife Sara was born three months premature, hardly larger than her father's hand. Nevertheless, she went on through her challenges within a rather extraordinary fifty-two-year life.

to be extinguished to safeguard another, then those medical necessities, by reason, must be exceedingly rare. Nevertheless, abortions remain extraordinarily common – even official in nations such as Communist China.

With so many innocent infants killed, one has to conclude that more than just politics or social equality remains at the apex. Even within the United States – where abortion ranks as the primary goal of aggressive leftist politics – it remains incredulous that mere 'rights' or 'medical care' could cause the wanton destruction (some horribly brutal in nature) of the most innocent human individuals. Yet, it happens. Again, *why*? The short answer remains: because some humans remain completely indifferent to their companions.

It takes a very strong imagination to view a newly born infant as a treasure to behold while viewing that same child, merely moments before, resting within the womb of the mother as any sort of organ or *non-human*. That, however, remains the argument of merit within domestic politics. One second, you are an inconvenient organ. The next, a viable human being worthy of state-centric medical care, free college education, and guaranteed income. So the Progressive/Socialist argument goes.

Unfortunately, abortion is not about rights or medical provision; it is *all* about population control, which is why the elitists within the world – entertainers, business leaders, scientists, etc. – are amongst its most enthusiastic endorsers. They seek to *dehumanize* people before they become overtly human in appearance so that they can decide precisely *who* is allowed to live within the world. And this, of course, is where we turn the discussion back towards professional killers.

People remain too diverse for them to consider a concrete comparison between an assassin's client determining who shall live and an abortionist's (defined herein as anyone who supports the practice) consideration of which vulnerable social classes to target. Spirits – both angelic (good) and demonic (bad) – are even more diverse, in that each is as different from one another as a gnat is from a wildebeest. Those that followed Lucifer as he was thrown out of Heaven are no exception, but their commonality is direct opposite to that which grants the proper angels their purpose: the demons remain in unison regarding the destruction of the human population.

Satanic demons, owing to their absolute opposition for the elevation of human beings above the created universe, attempt *every* measure to dilute not only the inherent value of *all human persons*, but adamantly seek to diminish their own role within the world. As initiators of the most ancient battle imaginable (Revelation 12:7-12, *New American Bible*), the demons remain the originators of militant deception and deceit. As pure intelligences, they remain masters of controlling both human thoughts and natural events. Therefore, their presence within the world – and our human reluctance to admit that presence – comes with the following covers:

- *Denial.* Satan and demons remain a figment of ancient human religious practices and do not portend to represent actual beings. Thoughts such as demonic possession are easily explained through psychiatric evaluation and social understanding;
- *Dilution.* Devils? Really? Science has already *proven* that everything must follow physics or biology. There is *nothing* that exists that cannot be quantified or qualified. Particle physics and the Big Bang prove beyond a reasonable doubt that theories of spirits remain little more than people trying to comprehend the infinitesimal – not our failure to consider the infinite.
- *Diffusion.* It's only music [or movies, or television, or books...], we are not endorsing satanic practices. Just because we enjoy

demonic movies does *not* mean that we endorse
satanism. Just like how we play "violent" video
games has absolutely *nothing* to do with any
desire to shoot up a school full of students or a
church full of congregants.

- *Diversion.* Hey, just look at those Christians [or
  Muslims, or Jews, or...]! They kill too! Don't
  suggest that my belief in the occult or
  supernatural is at fault. *Everyone* is equally at
  fault for crimes; I am just doing what *everyone
  else* is doing.

These four tactics keep demonic influence as little more than
an archaic caricaturization. They dispense with reality – in
the same manner that proponents of gun control believe that
new legislation will defeat armed crime – by distracting
attention away from facts.

In a similar manner, the professional assassin sees
his or her function as little more than a service, as befitting
any respectable doctor, attorney, or architect. Because their
purpose is to conduct the murder without anyone being wise
to their role within it, they do fret over apprehension or
prosecution in the manner that, say, Adolf Eichmann
constantly looked over his shoulder. Deaths happen every
day and that their target just happened to represent one of
these many deaths remains little more than a coincidence
that *nobody in authority* will ever cast a second glass
towards.

Again, to carry off such an orchestrated murder
requires an absolute disconnect with the rest of the human
population in the same manner as, say, a rancher butchering
"just one of the steers" existing upon his ranch. Whereas the
rancher may be feeding his family, so, too, may the
professional assassin. Each one's attention towards the duty
at hand rests within a particular judicial consideration. The
rancher, for example, may select his steer based upon age,
size, or expected meat production. Perhaps, even, the steer in

question was arbitrarily disposed of to reduce the herd.

Professional assassins rule by a sense of justice that remains unfathomable by most standards. A provision of death that exceeds the moral code determined by most civilized people and, yet, still retains a deeply unnerving discrimination beyond legal juncture. That is, a professional assassin will consider a heretofore unknown individual and then come to know that particular person better than had anyone ever within that target's life, and then judiciously decide whether or not to affect that individual's untimely death. And all for pay – little more (although challenge is inherent).

In a very broad sense, such assassins remain, again, little more than digital computers; they accept a contract, or they don't. This decision is based upon whether they can get away with the murder, or not. Even the pay for the act in question depends upon whether they can pull off the crime or not. More succinctly, his or her mind functions along parameters far more stringent and uncompromising than any other professional on the planet. Here is where, perhaps, diabolical evil reveals itself most profoundly.

The mindset of an independent, contract assassin cannot be discussed without the requisite of dismissing any thoughts of emotion or prejudice. Even a cursory examination of the evening news illustrates, for example, how extremely hateful politics in the modern world has become.[4] When people bear grievances, whether at work or in public, they *generally* react with vocalized output. That is, most people are quite willing to voice his or her public in a volume that meets his or her expectations, and then they go about their daily lives.

To the contrary, the independent killer may *only* appear politicized if it fits in with his or her cover.

---

[4] At the time of this writing, 2018, the United States is engaged within its midterm election cycle with proponents from both political spectrums leveling accusations of violence against one another with, perhaps, the Left leaning towards more open public endorsement of aggressive behavior.

**Figure 2. Layering of Human Mind.** Reproduced from Godlewski, R.J. "Human Intelligence: Perceiving an Enemy's Thoughts" in *American Intelligence Journal* 27, No. 1 (Fall 2009), 35.

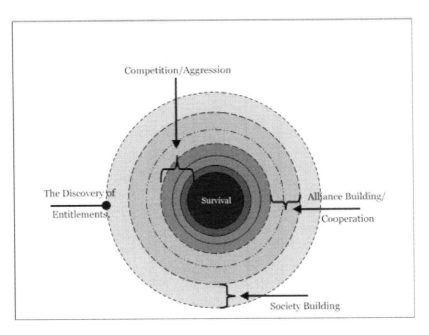

In Figure 2, we can observe how the human mind develops along onion layer matters of maturation and evolution. Everything founds upon survival and builds into societal concerns before passing into modernity's sense of relaxation and entitlement. Independent assassins, however, appear to have stalled within that nebulous boundary between competition and cooperation. That is, he or she is most happy to cooperate with their client's view of the world but prefer to remain within that cycle that keeps his or her work competitive, less they descend back into deeper aggression or wander into polite junctions frequented by the rest of the planet.

It is this inability – or, perhaps, reluctance – to move into society building that keeps the contract assassin in service. To foster any thoughts of social expectance means that he or she has to gauge their actions in relationship to that community. In other words, one cannot be focused on the good of society while killing people he or she had little choice in choosing outside elements of pay and opportunity. One cannot apply extreme justice while endorsing civic rule.

Despite the world's preference for wars – either declared or not – humans cannot accept death on an individual, fee basis. Perhaps we have become too immune to atrocities such as Darfur, Rwanda, Bosnia, etc. to consider people killing for either pay or sport alone. The latter location and insinuation offering a chance for the public to observe a facsimile, albeit one on a much larger, conflict wide basis.

The urban sniper campaign of 1992-1996 in Sarajevo, Bosnia-Herzegovina epitomized the worst that humanity has to offer itself, with Serbs shooting *anyone* – small children, pregnant women, elderly shoppers, even zookeepers – that appeared within the open.[5] The indiscriminate killing of Muslim Bosnians (and a few Catholic Croats) involved thousands of snipers, some of which were little more than sporting tourists and "weekend adventurers" that came to the city simply for the chance to shoot away at residents before returning to their schools, businesses, and family lives.

That *anyone* could kill on a part-time basis purely for the novelty of the "sport" lends credence to the effect of evil upon some individual's lives, but to kill seven-year-old children and young women underscores the absolute indifference some people hold for human value. Nevertheless, despite the seeming inability to place substance upon peoples' lives, the atrocity in Sarajevo resulted from simple hatred of the Serbs against other ethnic groups (and, later, those groups against the Serbs).

Reportedly, many of the Serb forces, including those

---

[5] For a technical analysis of this element of the conflict, see West, John. *Fry the Brain: The Art of Urban Sniping and its Role in Modern Guerrilla Warfare* (Countryside, VA: SSI, 2008) 238-265, especially 246-250.

conducting the sniper terroristic campaign against the city, attempted – in true political fashion – to place the blame for the atrocities upon the innocent victims, going as far as to declare that since they would not surrender or vacate their city, it was *they* who were to blame for the killing, *not* the Serb forces doing the actual shooting and shelling. Whereas their presence surrounding the city legitimately came from raw hatred of the Sarajevans, the fact that they placed exclusive blame upon the residents verified their indifference to those victims.

The Biblical parallels towards this manifestation of deferring culpability come from both the Old and New Testaments. In the Book of Genesis, the serpent tempts Eve with the question, "Did God *really* [emphasis added] tell you not to eat from any of the trees in the garden?"[6] Here we have both temptation *and* deceit at its most militant level. Satan knew full well that God hadn't restricted Adam and Eve from partaking of *all* vegetation within the garden; merely that which involved the Tree of Life. Eve, however, innocent and very much on the defensive, was confronted with the fact that *most* of the plants could be eaten so why not – as Satan implied – *all* the plants. Eve had simply been duped into exercising her nascent rationality and accepting blame for what the serpent offered.

In the New Testament, Christ Himself is tempted by Satan along similar lines, "*If* [emphasis added] you are the Son of God, throw yourself down from here for it is written: 'He will command his angels concerning you, to guard you' and: 'With their hands they will support you, lest you dash your foot against a stone.'"[7] Of course Christ *knew* that He was God, in human form, and so no proof was required from His perspective. That said, Satan – although an illustrious spirit, still unfathomably ignorant in comparison – attempted to harm the human body of Jesus while, perhaps,

---

[6] Genesis 3:1, *NAB*.
[7] Luke 4:9-11, *NAB*.

erroneously trying to cast human doubt into the human side of the Incarnate God.

The examples above show the archaic nature of people distancing themselves from responsibility for others' lives and the demonic presence amongst us that serves a ceaseless purpose in harming humanity as a whole and as many *individual* human lives as possible. Again, when time is of little consequence – as for those who hold neither corporeal presence nor limitations from physical laws of nature – there is no reason to squander on trying to destroy civilization en masse; one soul at a time would do rather convincingly.

Here, again, we are confronted with the assassin-client relationship. One lives within an idealistic world where individual human lives matter very little under the precept of satanic principles of practicality: "you can do what you wish, that is, without subjugation to God's laws; you obey no one; and you are the god of yourself."[8] In this regard, he or she values human life so little as to declare a particular person as unworthy of living. Accordingly, they believe that they can finance that individual's death (and escape culpability from that killing) regardless of God's – or man's – will, and they commit to do so because *they* matter most within the world. They have essentially made a covenant with Evil to play God.

The other individual, the independent assassin, merely serves as the architect and engineer of that procured death. They are not the serpent, necessarily, but the *apple* fouling paradise. In his or her estimation, their world is not idealistic, but interminably rational. Like Eve, or the Serb scandalization of Bosnians, it is *not the assassin* that is guilty of the more egregious sin, but the client *who partakes of the sin to gain greater pleasures*. The tree of modern life would still remain lush and vibrant if it were not for the self-serving clients who deem a killing as far more productive than letting the poor soul continue on. Or the assassin's

---

[8] Amorth, Gabriele Fr. and Stefano Stimamiglio. Translated by Charlotte J. Fasi, An *Exorcist Explains the Demonic* (Manchester, NH: Sophia Institute Press, 2016), 18.

thought process believes.

In a similar manner, many people consciously violate "minor" laws as befitting his or her needs. For example, a motorist may exceed the speed limit in order to arrive at work or the grocery store on time. They are, technically, breaking well established (and posted) laws, but they negate the legislation because it benefits them. Yet, should *they* be passed by another speeding automobile, they are quite likely to complain about the other's infraction of the same law.

Assassins and their clients behave in much the same way, if only with minor differences based upon which side of the equation they reside. The client, for instance, will see the target individual in the same manner as a speeding motorist observes another roaring past. The *other's* transgressions are wrong, because they affect his or her ability to navigate at will, despite their own violation of law and order. An investment banker may, as but one example, consider the murder of another because that offending individual's more aggressive tactics provide him with greater success. If one cannot lead the pack, one simply diminishes the herd.

As for the assassin, they do not see speeding cars as reasons to kill; rather, they observe traffic patterns for their potential to cause casualties. Whenever a motorist races past the assassin's car, he or she is not likely to response with expletives. On the contrary, they make quick mental notes of the driver and attempt to estimate his or her personality for future reference. If they can perceive enough similarities with a targeted individual, then "death by car accident" may avail itself. Or at least draw into a broader plan where an accident may open other opportunities for death.

Whatever the perceived reason behind the murder, its occurrence rests upon the client's determination that the targeted individual stands in the way of perceived progress. He or she is a threat to the client and, therefore, a sense of "justice" warrants his or her murder. They simply cannot be afforded the luxury of repenting for that violation.

# A TIME FOR A KILLING

EVEN BEFORE A contract is accepted by the assassin, a mental plan begins to materialize within his or her mind. During this period, they formulate patterns of behavior and personality regarding the target individual, learning as much about the subject person than most people devote towards their spouse within a lifetime of marriage. To effectively kill an individual and get away with the crime, several factors must be affected:

1.    The murder must be conducted during a period in which the victim's mannerisms suggest normalcy. For example, if the target dislikes the cold weather, it would be impractical to have them fall victim to a "freak skiing accident". Similarly, if they did not enjoy crowds, it would be equally disadvantageous to muster a death within the frightening masses. The effect here is to avoid anyone from considering *why* the helpless victim found him or herself within that predicament;

2.    The murder must be conducted within a manner that heralds "routine" or "accidental" to preclude thoughts of mechanization or artificiality. A person blown up at the mailbox raises red flags for miles. As would a body showered with bullet holes. On the other hand, few would suspect an elderly person with a heart condition suffering cardiac arrest. Nor would they second guess someone drowning within a swimming pool with an extremely high blood alcohol content – especially if that individual remained a known drinker.

3.    Finally, the murder cannot leave forensic evidence

behind to compromise either of the above two conditions. Unfortunately, a great many avenues of death – orchestrated or natural – leave telltale signs of the culprit. Even a simple act such as falling down the stairs can leave suggestions, such as a bruised toe, that hint at "something" causing the victim to undertake that fall. Poisons, explosives, firearms, bare hands, etc. all leave trace amounts of evidence whose detection rests merely upon the time and funding available to the authorities. To be successful, the assassin must employ the least number of artifacts along with the proper opportunity to destroy – rather than simply dispose of – that evidence (such as, say, using monofilament fishing line to trip the victim down a flight of stairs followed by melting the line for more expedient dispersal).

These considerations hint at something more sinister than the act of murder itself.

Acts are, by definition, the process of doing a thing. Legally, an act is further defined by the process of it being undertaken voluntarily. We can arbitrarily add a third dimension – whether the act remains good or bad in relation to normality. And "normality", here, rests upon what has survived the test of time – not necessarily, say, politics or popular opinion. In this regard, we are considering the context of thousands of years rather than mere decades.

Murder, as but the topic of discussion at the present, has been considered illegal, immoral, and completely evil for thousands of years. Only much more recently have people tried to legitimate the practice through an endless litany of grievances on behalf of the culprit. Nevertheless, the indiscriminate killing of another human being has always been viewed as outside the norm of society; only governments and militaries bore the sufficient jurisprudence to take others' lives. Therefore, the killing of an innocent remains murder; the killing of scores remains atrocity.

As for the act of assassination – especially if so ordered

by a private individual – the crime in question not only violates societal progress, it hampers human evolution. In the first regard, selectively targeting individuals for death without just cause simply "kills" contributions towards progress offered by that person. Even notoriously bad individuals benefit society if proper legislation arises from his or her actions. In the latter circumstance, assassination – by virtue of it representing a "catch me if you can" crime – thwarts human evolution by distorting humanity's progress towards seeking its Creator, as *all* humans were designed to do.

We must now elaborate on this a bit. Society requires that just laws surface outside the influence of political agenda. For example, slavery represents a nearly universal condemnation even if a great many countries still benefit from the practice. This is because human freedom – an inalienable right – ensures the progression of liberty despite governments best efforts to corral it (such as through enacting gun control) or diffuse it (by instituting "rights" that do not inherently exist, as with the case of abortion).

Along similar veins, human evolution mandates that individuals seek absolute happiness in order to survive. Compounding this reality remains that *most* humans seek happiness through temporal avenues of pleasure such as money, sex, drugs, and power. Nevertheless, these activities *never* generate lasting happiness – which can only be achieved through death and the realization that earthly life remains but a blip in the context of the universe. That is, from the theological perspective, people cannot find true happiness until they come face to face with God, the Creator of everything people desire.

It is within this context of earthly, or temporal, happiness that assassins emerge as bona fide elements of another's success. They exist solely to kill their victims so that his or her client can remove an obstacle towards happiness. By determining precisely – in so far as practical – *when* an individual will die, and thus end their own trek towards self-happiness, the client and assassin become deified in their own right. It is within their concept of *timing* the victim's death that transcends the earthly order.

Frankly, most individuals bear little thought regarding *kairos* time ("life" time such as the flow of a river or length of a pregnancy) and merely concern him or herself with *chronos* time, such as when they punch the clock at work or arrive at the airport. As such, very few people appreciate the complex patterns that humanity offers. In the modern world, we set our *chronos* watches to sporting seasons, election cycles, and lottery hopes, never minding that one cannot quantify *kairos* any more than one can determine human life without witnessing birth. Some things simply *are* whether we analyze them or not.

When a client orders an assassination, it specifically rests upon whether the event occurs or not and, largely, particularly *when* the client no longer needs to worry about his or her adversary – ever again. Their impatience may even cause them to gaze upon their watch throughout the day to consider if "today" is the day that the target dies. The assassin, for his or her role, cannot afford to worry about the ticks of a clock or the wonderings of a client. A killing occurs when everything is lined up correctly and all the gray areas have been voided out. The assassination simply becomes an *event* – one with its own lifespan and termination.

Inasmuch as people *cannot* know, precisely, when a human being is created (though we are getting close to determining the *chronos* of natural conception), an assassination does not arise from a simple handshake or even with a signed contract. There remain far too many factors involved between the client's insistence that their adversary should die and the killer's actual carrying out of the deed. In fact, neither may actually meet or communicate directly. In this regard, the commitment to kill and the "contract" flushing out the details blend into a life of their own. And here is where, once again, we observe the influence of demonic evil within the entire affair.

The client's personal determination to kill an offending

individual rests upon raw emotion, even if subconsciously. Emotions, however, are fleeting; no one – even your most psychotic individuals – can keep any one particular emotion going for longer than a few minutes at most. Instead, most adversarial people flow through cycles of greed, anger, lust, resentment, hatred, envy, and jealousy before they commit their act.

We can observe similar cycles within a love relationship, for instance. A couple may go through infatuation, friendship, concern, even obsession before they finally realize that their relationship over the years had simply been one of love and its many facets of intrigue. In the journey through *kairos*, there remain little chronological guideposts worthy of merit beyond the observations of hindsight.

To affect an assassination, the independent killer must focus upon both the *kairos* of the target's life and of the planned killing as well for each intersect. He or she must literally absorb *everything* that is knowable about the target, for to neglect any one detail may lead to failure and possible apprehension by the authorities. Frankly, ordinary people simply are not sufficiently focused enough to consider all these aspects of others' lives. Yet, independent assassins – necessarily working without *any* support network – are not ordinary.

To delve into the sinister mastery of the assassin's trade, we must continue to gaze into that which does not meet our eyes or arrive at our ears. In reading about the spiritual world – both angelic and demonic – we come to find that such spirits "...can introduce pictures into our imagination, they can reach into the storehouse of memory and parade the past before our mind's eye..." and they "...can suggest through imagination and memory, they can coax, entice, threaten, or frighten through these avenues of our sense nature; but we are the ultimate masters in command of our lives."[9]

For the non-theologian – or even persons of no religious faith whatsoever – the foregoing remains simple. *Every* individual on the planet faces the realities of images and memories for which he or she had little or no reason to bring up at the particular time that these thoughts arrived into their mind. In other words, people, from time to time, recall a memory or envision an image that, to them, seems completely out of character with what he or she was doing at that precise moment in their lives. If we assume that such reflections were not brought about by that individual's actions (say, seeing children play baseball in the street may conjure similar thoughts of the observer's youth), then something or *someone* external to his or her mind introduced that thought.

Now, taking this a step further. If we assume that whatever *willingly* created that thought also had access to the memories of other individuals, we can suspect that these images could be transposed from one person's mind to another, *without* that person effectively knowing about that action. Furthermore, a mind set free – by design or by genetics – from compassion and concern for the world around them could, conceivably, not be swamped with the myriad of emotions that keep the rest of the planet from paying too close attention to these artificial thought patterns. Might not such a mind be predisposed to absorbing all that information that an independent assassin requires to affect his or her trade?

It should be remembered that such "desensitization" is already rampant within the modern world as the entertainment and videogame industries progressively indoctrinate children into accepting sociopathic action

---

[9] Farrell, Walter and Martin J. Healy, *My Way of Life: Pocket Edition of St. Thomas, The Summa Simplified for Everyone* (Brooklyn: Confraternity of the Precious Blood, 1952), 72-73.

through extremely violent films and games.[10] Through these popular avenues, children and teenagers become immune to the realities of violent, almost absurd killing rituals. Can a parallel between the virtual and spiritual worlds exist and represent the root of this problem. Yes, of course.

St. Paul, for one, warns us of the battle against such an evil: "...our struggle is not with flesh and blood but with the principalities, with the powers...with the evil spirits in the heavens."[11]Principalities and Powers represent two of the famous nine choirs of angels (both good and bad spirits). Of the demons, their temptations assailed against humans come largely against our intellect and intelligence, most notably through the dilution of conscience.[12]

If one were convincing an individual to partake of assassination as a proprietor, there could be no easier way of achieving this goal than through elevating his or her intellect while diminishing their conscience. Intelligence tends to deify the mind and abandon the heart. Consider, "[in] 1975 Dr. Narut, a U.S. Navy psychiatrist...was developing [techniques] for the U.S. government in which classical conditioning and social learning methodology were being used to permit military assassins to overcome their resistance to killing."[13] These classical conditioning methodologies remain little different from the progression of children and teenagers through those ever more violent videogames and movies. Might not an evil spirit – especially the most intelligent and capable of them all – purse the same path of desensitization?

From here we can extrapolate the kind of mind that is required to spend months orchestrating an individual's death along with the extraordinary amount of information pertaining to that person's life required to affect an untraceable assassination. Almost in Hollywood fashion, the

---

[10] Grossman, Dave, *On Killing: The Psychological Cost of Learning to Kill in War and Society* (New York: Back Bay Books, 2009), 310-315.
[11] Ephesians 6:12, *NAB*.
[12] Amorth, *Exorcist*, 64-65.
[13] Grossman, *On Killing*, 310.

diabolical, independent and professional assassin acquires and compartmentalizes enough information about his or her targets to fill literally dozens of encyclopedias and formulates a strategy to kill those individuals as if merely an engineer, accountant, or attorney plying his or her trade.

The sheer amount of time required to collect this information – not to mention the act of ignoring most of this data once the killing has taken place – is, again, simply not a *human* endeavor. Inspiration, intelligence, and – for lack of better words – "moral" support has to come from an external source far more insidious than the killer. And this source "...was a murderer from the beginning..."[14] Someone who, incapable of tiring or growing weak, possesses the empirical knowledge and influence of every known killer from Cain on through the present.

To affect an assassination *professionally*, the independent contract killer literally wades into the life and happenings of the victim; spending weeks and months observing little else but the movements, mannerisms, and peculiarities of a *single individual*, looking for the right time, situation, and opportunity to, more often than not, permit that unfortunate individual to basically kill themselves through habit, weakness, or neglect. Anything that the victim does that can lead to his or her demise will be promptly used by the assassin in order to distance him or herself from the crime.

This *timing* of the assassination represents an extraordinary calculation, far beyond the limits of even the most gifted individual. Consider for instance, the actions of military special operations forces sent on hunter-killer assignments. They are largely supported by a range of intelligence, surveillance, and reconnaissance (ISR) assets, properly briefed by military leadership, and backed by innumerable military hardware, units, and personnel. An "individual" bears none of these things and, yet, more than a

---

[14] John 8:44, *NAB*.

few orchestrate unnerving killings throughout the planet. How they can carry out such crimes remains, literally, spiritual.

Scheduling, fabrication of hardware, safehouses and escape plans, all these things must be kept within the mind of a single individual – a superhuman effort if there ever was one. Imagine the chances for an Olympic athlete that bore no outside training resources or sponsorship other than his or her own initiative. One could conclude that he or she could not fathom any expectations of attending the Games, let alone winning a gold medal, but such is the realization of the assassin's world.

In a very real sense, the independent contract killer becomes not a human individual partaking of a routine career, but a sinister conduit for a more diabolical personage intending to destroy humanity one soul at a time. The killer then, becomes less free and more subject to the directions of evil; a mere sensor feed by the most horrendous data imaginable for mortal human beings.

Critics may scoff at the notion of spiritual influence, but the twin facts remain: independent assassins exist and their activities border upon the surreal. To kill repeatedly and not be caught remains the stuff of urban – and satanic – legend. For all its imagination, even Hollywood *cannot* reproduce the story without rapid gunfire, prerequisite torture, or blowing entire buildings up with fantastical pyrotechnics. Remaining true to the profession not only lacks entertainment, it reeks of simplicity of design.

Given the constraints of, say, a ninety-minute motion picture – even one with 21st century computer-generated imagery – there is not much profit in exposing the cerebral nature of the industry (though the satanic angle would probably whet the appetite of even the most squeamish producer). Assassinations taking weeks and months to plan leave too much to history for there to be any film worthy of note. Even when the killer arrives at that "aha" moment where a plan *might* be realized, several events – and cautious planning – prevent improvisation.

Absorbed into the victim's lifestyle and mannerisms, the assassin judiciously selects an opportunity that nativizes the death of that individual in such a manner as to foster inculpability for the crime. The killer, to keep the film analogy intact, prepares a mental script for the assassination, often marking new directions on the margins and always tearing out pages for due attention elsewhere (what might fail one assassination could come in handy for another).

Each step, each action, each consideration is played out as if a checklist for an airliner. Only when the mechanics and environment warrant, will he or she descend into the timetable that selects the *when* the killing will occur. Perhaps more so than any other feature of the crime, *timing* remains out of the hands of the assassin; he or she takes what circumstances and the victim provide.

# VIATICUM

DEATH IS ONLY a natural condition of the human species by virtue of Original Sin, theologically speaking. Today, we realize that death is part of the living process; as our bodies age, cellular functions decrease unto unsustainable limits. Ordinarily, this takes a great many years to accomplish, perhaps as much as one hundred. Nevertheless, the relatively weak human body is confronted with a myriad of diseases, poisons, and injuries that quickly shorten one's life expectancy to where, in 2018, an adult male or female may only reach seventy-five to eighty years of age. Added to these natural enemies of the body rests several artificial barriers, not the least of which remains external aggression.

Through one of several methods of interfering with the brain's control of the body, an individual may quickly bring about the death of another. The victim's life is snuffed out as quickly as pulling the electrical plug for a television or the battery for a cellular telephone. In other cases, life is not so easily drained, such as if power is interrupted to a laptop computer. In this case, a very limited "battery" keeps the brain anxiously trying to comprehend a way of communicating with the rest of the body. Here, those sensors "hardwired" directly into the brain – eyes, ears, nose, tongue, etc. – *may* still produce signals as the brain itself slowly dies from lack of oxygen.

Whether a murdered victim dies quickly or literally suffocates depends largely upon the approach taken by an assailant. A shotgun blast to the abdomen, for example, will quickly kill a person, but not before he or she realizes what has happened and, likely, gazes upon his or her attacker with disbelief. Even a decapitated head may still be able to envision its murderer, but it remains suspected that such an emancipated part would be assailed with innumerous electrical impulses to fashion what the reader may recognize as true observation. The same holds true for those who take a high-powered bullet to the head; reports abound where sniper victims course through the ground as if, literally, misguided souls zigzagging for an unknown destination.

As with the analogy of the computer, the human mind, along with its central processing unit of the brain, is designed to "power down" within specific limits: the aging process referred to above. Anything that circumvents this evolutionary process remains detrimental to the health and wellbeing of the human spirit. Yet, as widespread as it appears to be, such actions against human neighbors is *not* a routine function of any person. Figure 2 suggests that aggression remains too buried into the psyche for "entitlement-driven" individuals to buck the trend.

What, then, are we to make of Dr. Stanley Milgram's Yale University studies during the late 1960s that proved that sixty-five percent (65%) of the world's population could kill with little more prompting than from an "authority figure" in a white lab coat?[15] How can people so averse to death remain so susceptible to killing? Again, the answer lies in the forces behind the thought; that which answers the question rests within *who* or *what* keeps an otherwise rational and peaceable individual on 'kill mode' throughout his or her life.

If a scientist working within a laboratory can induce a subject to torture an innocent "victim" through perceived authority, then what could a force impose that understands the very thought processes of an individual as well as that person's entire litany of fears, desires, associations, and heritage? Could someone who understands the very essence of an individual's character be considered, perhaps, the ultimate *authority*? For this, we must retreat back to the discussion of hatred versus indifference.

An axe murderer, for instance, remains a despicable

criminal with little regard to human compassion or valuation. Yet, the very nature of his or her crime rests with raw emotion. The act of literally hacking another to death is *not* a deliberate, calculated function by any stretch of the imagination. Whatever causes that person to kill builds up over a period of time until he or she can no longer appreciate the free will inherent within themselves and in a fit of rage, they turn upon (largely) whomever crosses his or her path.

Some individuals – admittedly acting within the days prior to modern forensic structure – have committed egregiously emotional crimes and yet disappeared into the notoriety of history. Britain's infamous Jack the Ripper remains, perhaps, the most illustrious example.[16] What makes the Whitechapel crimes so critical, however, is that while the Ripper killings were amongst the most horrific in human history, the murderer's actions still presented a profound appreciation of planning, communication, and even mocking with the local press. They were, at once, undertaken through a soul tormented with evil genius and the spontaneity of a true madman. The operative word here remains *evil* genius.

Only one well-versed within the environment of Whitechapel and its many inhabitants and their mannerisms could have retreated from the crimes without apprehension. Few individuals can accomplish this. Contrast this with the case of Charles Joseph Whitman who systematically shot forty-six people at the University of Texas in Austin during August 1966.[17] This latter case involved nearly all of the elements of the Whitechapel murders – an intuitive understanding of the environment, an appreciation for how the local citizens went about his or her day, proper dress (i.e.,

---

[15] Grossman, *On Killing*, 141-142.
[16] Ogan, Jonathan and Laurence Alison, "Jack the Ripper and the Whitechapel murders: a very Victorian critical incident" in ed. Laurence Alison *The Forensic Psychologist's Casebook: Psychological Profiling and Criminal Investigation* (New York: Routledge, 2005), 23-46.
[17] West, *Fry the Brain*, 177-188.

camouflage) for the situation, etc. – with the exception that Whitman was ultimately killed and identified. Had the Texas crime happened a century earlier, it is possible that the gunman's actions would have disappeared into Ripper-like folklore.

Given these two examples, particularly the former, one has to consider the abject evilness of the actions, especially the ease in which Jack the Ripper walked away from any culpability for the crimes. Generally, people do *not* act so confidently. At least singular examples; nearly all the "well-orchestrated" crimes of history entail some form of conspiracy. And this is where our attention is immediately drawn back towards the independent contract assassin – another individual sinister enough to kill while possessing the panache to walk away from the crime with *zero* chance of apprehension.

Given the ability of certain individuals – the subject independent contract assassins operating outside any prominent external support – to consciously kill without it affecting any other aspect of his or her life (especially when many function "normally" within otherwise civilized society), one has to consider the onset of functional and/or simulated amnesia.[18] Here we have several paradoxes, most notably the ability for one to generate 'memory failure' when his or her job rests upon the primal ability to recall facts and figures at will. Another involves the understandable inconsistencies involved with any form of amnesia resulting from neither injury nor stress (assassins *having* to function reliably under a great deal of stress).

Perhaps, however, *another* mechanism for amnesia-like occurrences surfaces within the minds of professional killers. Here, we are largely discussing the ability of external, spiritual influences to cover, conceal, or diminish certain

---

[18] See Alison, Laurence, "Malingering or memory loss in a major collision investigation: reconstructing accounts of suspects, victims and witnesses." in ed. Laurence Alison *The Forensic Psychologist's Casebook: Psychological Profiling and Criminal Investigation* (New York: Routledge, 2005), 297-314.

aspects of that individual's thought processes. For example, if one were able to draw upon an individual's memory and foster both imagination and mental images, could not such a party alter self-perception of criminal acts? That is, could not such a creature fully dilute the actions of the contract assassin over the course of time to instill upon him or her a complete disregard for the crime they had planned and carried out?

Without getting too far into the abstract world of theology, we *can* attribute this ability to the unseen world of demonic spirits (or influences for the non-religious reader). We can observe this, partially, in an arena where almost everyone has taken note at one time or another: politics. Long gone are the days, it seems, where minor differences of effort characterize one political party (especially within the U.S.) over another. Today, the ideological differences between Left and Right are far more noticeable than in the past, say, with the perceived differences between communism and national socialism (i.e., Nazis).

In the modern era (2018), politicians and their pundits routinely criticize the opposition over completely false and unassociated issues. These individuals simply cannot foster *any* form of debatable differences, merely tuning out facts and truth for advantage. The progressive left, for instance, launches hysterical assaults on voters while simultaneously attempting to curry their support. Those that do not agree with them or snap to their beliefs are often marginalized in the most bigoted ways possible. Yet here, again, we are dealing primarily with emotions. The subject at hand, however, is meant to illustrate that some individuals can carry out relatively normal lives while his or her mindset remains fixed upon a very unnatural view of the world.

To kill for hire, and to do so repeatedly, is most emphatically *not* normal. Even Cain – Biblically humanity's first ever murderer and therefore fully immune to the heretofore nonexistent crime – expressed deep regret for the murder: "My punishment is too great to bear. Since you have now banished me from the soil, and I must avoid your presence and become a restless wanderer on the earth...”[19] Could he regret what had *never* happened before unless it was an inherent human trait for repentance? Even today, one cannot dream what one had never experienced, so one cannot regret that which had never occurred.

In this regard, we must consider, no matter how seemingly inconsequential, whether independent assassins bear a mechanism for controlled or selective amnesia. That is, if one does *not* hold regret for, perhaps, dozens of killings – and the time spent analyzing and planning for them – within his or her lifetime, *could* it be that, mentally, they had never before committed such crimes? Could a human person be so sinister as to commit murder after murder and actually *believe* that each is, say, a one-off act thereby diminishing the shock that other people would hold to the intentional taking of another's life?

If we build upon this narrative, then we *must* continue to view the subject matter under external, diabolical – if not openly demonic – influence. *Something* offers private assassins an ability to conduct surveillance and analysis on a victim for months before proceeding to orchestrate that person's untimely death in a manner that keeps authorities at bay under prolonged thoughts of "accidental" or "natural" demise. Unfortunately, mere *humans* are not that capable.

Governments and criminal groups bear legions of hierarchal authority and, in the case of the latter, daisy chain and wheel networks to divert attention and offer cut-outs to foster security. Even the John F. Kennedy assassination, allegedly the sole accomplishment of Harvey Oswald, now has rational experts suspecting that as many as thirteen parties were involved within the direct effort.[20] Whether one believes within a broader JFK conspiracy or not, everyone must consider the seeming impossibility of a single, largely untrained and emotional subject carrying out, perhaps, one

---

[19] Genesis 4:13:14, *NAB*.
[20] West, *Fry the Brain*, 153-176.

of history's most notorious crimes without any support.

Independent assassins, however, never aim for such public targets; there just is no longevity in changing the course of history forever. To kill a president, prime minister, pope, or anyone else of similar magnitude is not only unconscionable, it remains self-defeating and suicidal. Meaning, of course, that only those individuals who are either psychotic or emotional do carry out these crimes of hatred (where, as the adage states, an assassin becomes as famous as the victim). No single assassin would dare spend the rest of his or her life looking back over their shoulder as an entire planet of private investigators and amateur historians write about what they believe *really* happen. At some point, even the most notorious theory turns out correct.

Delving deeper into the independent assassin's mind, we have come to several prominent realizations that *cannot* be dismissed as unreasonable:

    ✓ *An extraordinary level of compartmentalization.* To fully exploit when, where, and how to kill a victim, an assassin bears upon him or herself a vast mental database of mannerisms, habits, experiences, peculiarities, and environmental considerations to affect such a murder. Once the present assassination is carried out, all this information is blocked out of the killer's mind *unless* a pertinent technique or mechanism is duly warranted again (herein the killer risks exposure by duplicating a tactic). It remains doubtful, for comparison, that an accomplished novelist, say, can forget the entirety of his or her writing over the course of the years. Nor is it reasonable to assume that *any* writer could forfeit his or her trademark style.

    ✓ *An absurd level of mental processing.* To process untold billions of facts and figures sufficiently well to compartmentalize them diminishes any comparison to the world's most modern artificial supercomputer. No mechanical device imaginable today bears the same raw initiative and common sense as the human mind. None. Yet, independent assassins expand upon this to a height of clarity and accuracy that even the "normal" human brain cannot emulate. Again, we are talking about a *singular* individual that literally carries an encyclopedic reference manual of *each* murder within his or her mind for the duration.

✓ *A total indifference for human value.* This aspect of the independent assassin can *never* be underestimated or over discussed. They are killing an individual that the assassin has spent weeks and months coming to know better than any spouse or confidant; an individual for whom they know about children, friends, and acquaintances; an individual where *they* – the independent assassin – decides when their dreams and ambitions effectively end. And, yet, they proceed to murder this victim without the slightest regret for his or her action.

✓ *A concrete policy of self-preservation.* Most people do not comprehend how relatively "lucky" they remain when it comes to personal survival. Almost *everyone* tempts providence in, say, speeding along the highway, visiting bars in high crime areas, and, perhaps, smoking while fueling their vehicles. People often survive by the skin of their teeth. Not so the professional assassin. Every moment of his or her existence gives away their primal instinct for survival. Every thought, every action undertaken as but one purpose: longevity, whether keeping abreast of their career, returning home safely, or simply going about routine affairs without fear of apprehension or incarceration.

These factors propel the independent assassin far past the merely "human" into something much more sinister.

To spend as much time transfiguring life and death is, perhaps, the greatest attribute that separates the independent contract killer from the remainder of society – including its more generic criminal elements. Their role, simply put, is to deliver death unto another and, by extension, however perverted it may be, "life" onto another soul. The trading of life for death and death for life as it were. Here, unfortunately, is where we impart politics into the equation once again.

Within its broadest application, politics represents the art and science of governing relationships between people living in society. In our discussion there remain three relationships that we need to address. First, there is the relationship between the client and the victim. Second, the relationship between the client and the independent assassin. Finally, we observe the relationship between the assassin and the target (Figure 3).

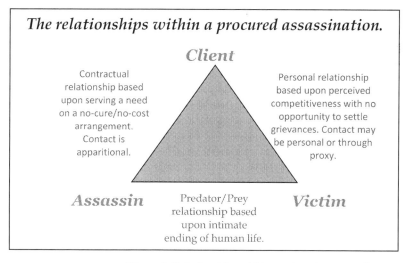

**The relationships within a procured assassination.**

Client

Contractual relationship based upon serving a need on a no-cure/no-cost arrangement. Contact is apparitional.

Personal relationship based upon perceived competitiveness with no opportunity to settle grievances. Contact may be personal or through proxy.

Assassin

Victim

Predator/Prey relationship based upon intimate ending of human life.

Figure 3. Relationships within a privately procured assassination.

The client governs the first relationship by determining that the latter must face certain death through self-perceived grievances and intentions. Accordingly, the client arbitrarily determines that the victim *must* die, and that said client must shield him or herself away from culpability with the crime. There is no justification for the decision other than that the intended victim sits in the direct path of the client's happiness – however that is defined. The relationship is personal, but there may be no *direct* interaction between the client and the targeted victim.

The second relationship exists between the client and the independent assassin, and basically represents a 'no-cure/no-cost' business arrangement where the assassin provides a service and the client funds it upon its successful conclusion. Despite the overtly sinister nature of the business, it is dealt with as confidentially as, say, an overseas financial transaction (which, it very well could be). Due to the nature of the offering, it is very rare that both client and assassin would be in direct communications with one another.

The final relationship represents the predator/prey interaction between the assassin and the victim. This is a deeply personal relationship for both the effort into the affair that the assassin provides and, of course, its final outcome. Generally, there is no direct contact between the parties, but the assassin may, with discretion, penetrate the victim's inner circle to include, but not be limited to, the target's home, family, business, and other social activities. Whatever it takes to gain advantage over the victim – while permitting the assassin an opportunity to duck responsibility for the crime – the contract killer will employ.

These relationships speak of undeniable brutality and evil; thrusting both innocence and criminality into commerce and socialization. Two parties conspiring against an ignorant – even, perhaps, naïve – person also brings elements of asymmetrical warfare into the equation. It represents a life and death struggle where one individual (rarely, groups) plays God, determining the worth of another individual whom he or she has elected to have killed. Without the decency of carrying out the crime firsthand, this individual sends out a professional killer, an independent assassin to target the victim and then leave grieving family and friends to assume that it was all a "freak accident" or a terribly injury never understanding that a competitor orchestrated the whole event.

The assassin becomes a conduit for this evil manifestation of pride and greed (of what else could it be when someone decides to have another killed?), a literal anointing of the soon-to-be deceased. Their role, after extensive and exhausting pre-mission surveillance and analysis, is to carry death unto an unsuspecting party and retreat into the netherworld of criminality on the run. One cannot appreciate this latter element of their trade enough.

Despite there being some six thousand unsolved homicides within the United States alone each year, most of these are attributed to situations where the victim warrants little consideration such as with the homeless, prostitutes, migrants, vagrants, etc. That anyone would pay hundreds of thousands to millions of dollars to have any of them killed is not realistic. Therefore, a contract assassin's target remains persons of merit, even if their death would not attract the attention of the media should their killing be determined as a homicide.

It remains the personal, yet seemingly "innocent" nature of the assassination that heralds great evil from the knowledgeable public. People can almost understand – though definitely not excuse – violent gang-related deaths as those in Chicago. Extraordinarily more violent deaths, such as those narcotics related occurrences in Mexico, are equally understood even if they belong "over there" in the minds of the television news watching population. Just about anything else conjures up images worthy of videogames and Hollywood action movies.

The planned and well-orchestrated *professional*

assassination, however, largely because of its nature, unnerves most citizens if they are observant enough to acknowledge the practice. With upwards of 85% of the United States, for example, subscribing to some monotheistic beliefs, this is quite understandable. People generally believe that killing is best left to *legitimate public authority* and death the sole domain of God.

For a private citizen to proffer the killing of a complete stranger (at that time) and to contract with another private citizen to affect this killing is beyond the imagination of ordinary people. Even within this violence intoxicated and therefore desensitized world, *private* killing remains abhorrent. When mass shootings, for instance, occur, individuals find it easier to either blame the availability of firearms or, even, to suggest orchestrated conspiracy.

Anything that permits the "rational" mind to dismiss the notion of clandestine killers within our midst makes the subject of independent assassins easier to cast aside as utter fantasy or the realm of government influence. Even corporate security and intelligence professionals mock the existence of individuals so crafty in their diabolical crimes as to render any discussion irrelevant. For them, if it does not follow cleared government regulations or industry certifications, it is not in existence.

# ABSENTE REO

TO CONSIDER THAT which is not easily observed, one must turn to rather obscure avenues of approach, many of which violate the rules set forth by scientific method. Thousands of years prior to the invention of the printing press and centuries before written language, people passed down stories and histories of remarkable accuracy. In those prewritten days, one's word was often valued as if gold. This was especially the case with scribes and other public officials whose livelihood (if not lives) depended upon getting the facts correct prior to disseminating them.

Today remains a different age when truth and fact give way to innuendo and hyperbole; when professionalism and investigation give way to cronyism and diversion. Artificial cliques and overt social classification make any discussion of independent contract assassins a subject to be ridiculed. And for good reason, the critics say. Independent assassins are *not* a viable species; there are no such people around to interview. This is, of course, the critics' challenge to the subject – one best left to the pages of best seller novels.

Nevertheless, Hollywood rolls in a great deal of money regarding contract killers, but they always miss the point on the matter. Their efforts focus on entertainment and pyrotechnics rather than realism. Movies such as *Sicario* (2015) broach the subject as always gray, always violent, always government-centric. The first thought dismisses the black and white nature of good versus evil, the second dismisses the extraordinary care professionals employ to *avoid* neighborhood-shaking assassinations, and the third dismisses that private enterprise remains much more efficient than bureaucratic governments.

A comparison can be made about Hollywood's other fascination with the spiritual world. In its "ghost" movies, the spirits are always omnipresent, supernatural, and as magical as yet another *Harry Potter* installment. In reality, spirits obey the same laws of nature as do humans. That they bear no corporeal existences does not imply that they are surreal; merely that they are not subject to time and physical relations with the natural world. Humans are, for instance, *present* wherever he or she is standing. Spirits are present wherever they are *acting* upon something. To suggest that angels and demons do not exist because they cannot be located within a particular "space" – space representing a *physical* nature – remains as absurd as suggesting that an individual's thoughts must exist in whichever environment they currently reside within.

To adequately write about the spiritual world, one must adequately detach one's thoughts from the physical. To write about independent contract assassins, similarly, one must detach themselves from the conspiratorial; from the rank and file of convention. To write about vipers, the saying goes, one must venture into the wild. To write about assassins, one must venture into some of the most notorious places on the planet. And not all of these are active war zones or Third World hellholes.

Many people would be amazed to realize just how close evil comes to their front door. Atlantic, Iowa, for instance, represents just one of the hundreds of smaller agricultural communities that dot the breadbasket of America. A town where the local Walmart Supercenter represents its primary employer. Yet, this relatively quiet town swarms in methamphetamines and human trafficking. One recent bust representing the latter netted some 300 Asian girls forced into prostitution according to former officials. Atlantic could be *any town*, however.

Larger urban centers tend to view crime as an existing problem and deal with the matter on a perennial basis. Honolulu, for one, has seen something of a growing pain from its Cold War days as a KGB-CIA battlefield. Where once conservative might fought against communist tyranny, the city (and state) now represent the bastion of liberal, progressive thought. The CIA helped beat the Soviet Union, but the KGB helped beat conservatism in the island capital and crime took on a more Triad basis than government influenced.

Global crime, wherever one resides, no longer fits into the mold of classification. One may function within narcotics, for example, but narcotics rests within financial crimes, prostitution, human smuggling, weapons trafficking, extortion, and a host of other vices too numerous to recite here. That one individual may farm coca leaves in Bolivia, another operating a refining lab in Colombia, a third a transportation hub in Mexico, and a fourth a sales territory in Phoenix does not dismiss that all are incorporated into the narcotics trade as a profession. Similarly, a human smuggler in Guatemala is no more or less culpable in illegal immigration as a liberal politician in Washington that espouses porous borders and sanctuary legislation.

To view life as either pastels or grays remains deceptive, for there is only yes or no, fact or fiction, truth or lie within the world. The number "1", for instance, can be broken down into innumerable fractions, but the whole digit *still* retains its presence. One cannot change the number without taking *something* away or adding to it; either addition or subtraction destroys the original value. Nevertheless, people are *always* seeking to change things for either convenience or benefit.

Consider again the oft-debated situation of illegal immigration. People either enter a country legally or they do not. There can be no other consideration without adding to or subtracting from, the original problem. In the first option, proponents may, for instance, add requests for asylum or social justice in order to get others to perceive some less than criminal effort behind the trend. These trespassers now become martyrs of sorts, fleeing ravages at home. In the second option, the one of taking something away, supporters may dilute the concept of national borders or try to eliminate enforcement of existing laws. Where everyone could agree to and accept the number "1", we now are confronted with either ½ or 1.75 instead.

The same holds true for the abomination of abortion, defined as the prevention of human life through the sacrifice of the fetus. Very few individuals, today, could accept the killing of an infant, for such is widely considered, perhaps, the most horrendous of crimes. Proponents of abortions, however, focus upon the same addition-or-subtraction method of deceiving others into accepting his or her own beliefs. They may, as one example, proclaim the self-perceived "right" to procure an abortion or address the issue of the "life of the mother" as being more important. Such tactics *add* to the underlying reality. Other insinuations, as with declaring the unborn infant as *merely an organ of the woman's body* tend to subtract from the realization that that "mere organ" is, in fact, a slowly developing human person.

Discussions on independent, contract assassins follow much the same parallels of including or removing key components of the profession. Discussion is simply not possible, the arguments rests, because there are so many killers on the planet, both from government and private sources, that independent assassins just cannot exist (addition). Conversely, there is no way that *anyone* can write about the subject because, as inherently covert operatives, no one can *approach* private assassins to learn about his or her trade (subtraction). And, by extension, one cannot write about Satan because that involves complex theological and historical tales too numerous to be believed (addition) and, well, he *doesn't exist* (subtraction) anyway.

Truth and facts, unfortunately, are not as indefinable as most would have you believe; facts being what is known and truth representing the correct interpretation of reality. In other words, the *fact* remains that the sky is either blue, cloudy, or black depending upon the time of day and climatic conditions, but the *truth* remains that the atmosphere itself is transparent. However we perceive the sky (fact) does *not* diminish the truth that, frankly, we can only observe *through* the sky, not itself as a whole. That is, when we gaze upwards we can observe, literally, for thousands if not millions of light-years in distance if we are not confronted with a solid mass or human limits on vision.

We can now assume several facts relating to our discussion:

- Some people kill.

- Some people kill *repeatedly*.

- Some people that kill repeatedly do so for *monetary gain*.

- Some people that kill repeatedly for monetary gain do so *as independent businesspersons*.

Facts, accordingly, lead to systematic realizations.

Now, we can broach the truth about the above statements:

> If someone people kill more than others and may even kill repeatedly for profit as private entrepreneurs, then *something* provides them with both the desire and the mindset to organize such a business pursuit.

Herein is where we must consider what, precisely, that *something* is. Logically, that "something" must either be artificial or natural; mechanical or theoretical. If we work on the assumption that it must be artificial, then we can equally promote that it must be mechanical, because theoretical subjects tend to flow from a person's *natural* imagination. On the other hand, natural things can spring from *both* mechanical (e.g., celestial) or theoretical processes.

Statistically, therefore, people cannot kill *repeatedly* from artificial stimulants (even drunks are sober part of the time) and this leaves us with fully natural reasons why professional assassins kill for a living.

Yet, *what* could be the 'natural' reason for his or her profession. Money? Excitement? Security? Money is only valuable when it is spent or otherwise utilized (e.g., as collateral). Excitement remains relatively fleeting. And nobody wants to kill for a living to remain secure within his or her life. Truthfully, there is absolutely no legitimate reason why independent assassins ply his or her trade – at least *internal* reasons.

Externally, there are numerous options to confront the would-be assassin: government control, criminal conspiracy, and, of course, those much-debated evil spirits. The first two options have been previously dismissed as confrontational to the independent proprietor and the third could, conceivably, be universal in that *all three* avenues remain subjected to unseen evil forces. Regardless, we shall concentrate on the latter; the solitary example that covers the very concept of private killers.

From start to finish, from childhood on through death, the entire career of the independent, professional, full-time (inasmuch as can be accommodated) assassin rests completely *within that individual's mind*. Here, at last, we are descending upon both the truth and the facts of the matter. All five of our senses are hardwired to observe only that which *we* have trained them to observe. For example, one person's "orange" may appear fundamentally different if viewed through another's perspective. We only know that orange is, indeed, orange by forcing ourselves to communicate with others. Otherwise, *everything* within the context of the human mind remains a product of that person's brain.

Marketing specialists may, for instance, promote that the latest cell phone as vastly superior than anything else on the market and that you *should* invest the hundreds of dollars necessary to purchase the device, but the ultimate decision comes down to the individual buyer's *will*. Some bear a stronger will and thus move on from the purchase. Others, weaker in spirit, fall for the ploy and shell out $900 to replace the $800 cell phone they purchase only six months prior.

Left uninjured and uninfluenced, the human mind develops into those outer 'onion layers' of evolution that promote cooperation and entitlement (Figure 2). "Most" people simply do not kill one another. According to Dr. Milgram's studies, a significant 35% of the population cannot be induced to kill *under any circumstances*. Yet, allowances must be made for a percentage – tiny, yes, but there nonetheless – of the population that can kill *without others knowing about it* (even clients really do not know the methods employed and, by extension, whether the assassin truly killed the victim).

What, then, *can* influence an independent professional's mind? Anything that employs that individual's memory, experiences, perceptions, and intellect. In other words, anything and everything that filters into that person's rational mind. The greater the person's will, however, the less likely they are to be influenced by outside forces – *unless those forces are stronger, more intellectual, and command a better recollection of that individual's life*.

Here is where we go back to the diabolical; demons that understand a person better than that person knows him or herself. It is within this context that we separate the merely murderous (i.e., the emotional) from the cold, calculating mind (i.e., the indifferent) of the private assassin. Unlike the former that may be induced into killing for notoriety, revenge, or obedience, the latter bears ultimate responsibility for his or her own actions.

The independent assassin just may represent the planet's only true *non-human* homo sapiens. That is, individuals resting outside the normal social, communicative, and environmentally conscious aspects of his or her neighbors. Without the ability to concern themselves with assimilation, no desire to communicate with bonded relationships, and, above all, no ability to consider an environment as anything more than a transient habitat, these individuals forfeit any semblance to human people. And herein rests their sole Achilles' heel.

On a daily basis, assassins are little more than actors – albeit on an immeasurably horrific scale. As persons of eternal "cover" and deception, they cannot allow themselves to fall back upon any degree of normalcy. Their lives in, say, Oregon remain exceedingly different than their personalities when touring France or Japan. They are the masters of social disconnect; emotion long since drained from their early lives. Because of this, independent assassins do not always hide his or her opinions even if they shield their lives with the greatest of intensity. A talented chef, say, may never reveal his sacred recipes, but crumbs are always there for the observant.

In life, very few can go about his or her daily life without noticeable habits, opinions, or actions. These traits announce specific personalities as if a parade, almost to the point of disappearing into the background noise of billions of other personalities. People just do not waste time and energy concealing themselves. From a distance, this sea of otherwise unique individuals blends into a tapestry of chaos and disorder as if a cluttered freeway during rush hour. Few even bother to notice until an accident appears or someone else provides a disruption to the erratic flow of conformity.

Deception takes energy. Security takes energy. Concealment takes energy. Success takes energy – a great deal of it. All of this bears upon the human mind and assassins remain no different. As with military veterans – or even mercenaries of old – one can observe another professional in a moment's notice. How? Because the one thing that humans *are* good at, even if he or she fails to realize the situation, is adhering to Darwin's law that the closer two species are to one another, the greater their confrontation for primacy will be.

This is *not* to say that professional assassins are so numerous as to jockey about for recognition. On the contrary; the statement is made that certain traits of the independent killer remain similar to a great many other, more respectable, professionals. For example, politicians are merely salespeople. They will tell you what *you want to hear* and partake of activities that *you normally endorse* merely to close the deal and have you "purchase" their wares. Once out of the store – or voting precinct – you never hear from them again.

The same holds true with determining which visitors to a gallery are fellow artists – professional or amateur – simply by hearing their criticisms. Generally, ordinary visitors do not spend much time critiquing colors, strokes, or even the perceived intentions of the creator. As such, these individuals reveal as much through their analyzes as does the artwork reveal the personalities of the artists.

Assassins – even independent ones – talk, as do all people. Most bystanders, however, never bother to listen let alone comprehend the idiosyncrasies being revealed. Moreover, many of these indications only suggest themselves long after the fact, when even the most appreciative person recollects the mysterious soul that "got away" before a million questions could have been asked. As with the proverbial ghost in the mist, an encounter with a professional assassin cannot herald any great notoriety, but the passage of the personality does reveal a good deal about their trade and his or her role within it.

As with a singular piece to a large jigsaw puzzle, the tiny object holds no remarkability in itself. All that truly *can* be determined, is that it remains little more than a piece to a puzzle. Even if one image upon it bears recognition, such as an animal or vehicle, one cannot address whether the larger image is of a park or the wild, of a street or a city. In the same way, we can discover pieces of great evil within the world, but we never know if this is the work of Evil (i.e., the

Devil) or simply an evil-minded individual (pleasing to Satan, naturally, but wholly orchestrated by that person's will).

Even today's intelligence analysts and political pollsters often misread the facts and fail miserably. As society becomes more in tune to technology and data mining, we are losing the ability for perception and clairvoyance. Gone is the ability to determine – as with nineteenth century gunslingers and gamblers – and perceive any enemy's thoughts.[21] While not fully necessary for survival – today – such capabilities allow us to siphon information away from others that may not be forthcoming from those who surround us.

We can learn how individuals respond to stimuli that speak of unusual careers, such as observation of surroundings, reactions to critical noises, and whether they pay attention to emergency exits and protective barriers. We may even observe how he or she responds to emergencies and whether *that* suggests a level of knowledge foreign to his or her *purported* career. Finally, we may be able to see how indifferent that person truly is from concern for his or her fellow companions upon this planet.

None of this, of course, heralds the existence of a professional killer. For that, we must delve deeper into the human psyche and learn more from others – particularly those clients who may have long since abandoned their allegiance to the community of silence. Certainly, as non-professionals within the killing department, clients will ultimately talk, even only to keep their graces with his or her Creator when the time comes to set the record straight (or as straight as they care to admit). However this information flows, it *does* flow – even if only in trickles.

People talk more through Captain Morgan's® influence then they do through a prosecutor's. Others can be "persuaded" to reveal details they possess if the investigator is more interested in the truth than legality. Then there

---

[21] See Godlewski, R.J. "Human Intelligence: Perceiving an Enemy's Thoughts" in *American Intelligence Journal* 27, No. 1 (Fall 2009), 29-37.

remains the "convenience factor"; just *how* convenient is it for a drunk to mount a horse and go galloping off until he meets his demise. And the "accident factor"; people who gain great wealth and influence generally do not trip down stairs, though they do fall victim to mysterious illnesses.

Assassins, representing people, do come in varying degrees of proficiency, as would be expected of attorneys, doctors, and tax accountants. They do speak, even if the words come from those not directly controlling their mouths. Sometimes, information regarding independent assassins comes from implications received from their more organizational brethren such as government-sponsored or narcotics related assassins. Here, the astute investigator may simply deduce the failures of these two groups and consider how *others* may bypass the errors.

Independent assassins and demonic spirits share numerous attributes that make the discussion all the more rational, if not believable by the non-religious. Their influence is real, their presence indeterminable, and their goal one of absolute destruction. That we may never catch evil spirits "red-handed" does not mean that they do not exist any more than saying that because no independent assassins are convicted means they do not exist either. We just may be looking in the wrong location or anticipating what may not be directly observed.

Our discussion here has been exclusively dealing with such evil influence upon the individuals who contract out as private assassins and their clients. These are real entities and not merely fictional elements of Hollywood horror movies. Evidence towards this is offered throughout human history, but we shall retain a singular reference from the Biblical record.

The confrontation between the demon "Legion" and Jesus underscores two important facts. First, the name of the demon suggests a possession from a very large number of spirits (at that period, a Roman legion consisted of between

5,000 and 6,000 foot soldiers).[22] Second, Jesus – at the
demon's own insistence – cast the lot into nearby pigs.[23] This
proves that evil spirits are *not* abnormal psychological
thoughts; they are real and capable of infecting both humans
and animals. Another noteworthy case involves St. Peter's
rescue from Herod's prison by an angel.[24] Spirits – both holy
angels and evil demons – can cause individuals to fall asleep,
remove shackles, and open locked doors, not to mention tap
a sleeping saint upon the shoulder. Certainly, they persuade
other individuals to kill with uncanny abilities.

It should be mentioned, especially, that such
knowledge of the influence of demons is *not* restricted to
Biblical times for the author of this text witnessed first hand
the ability of such spirits – again, both good and bad ones –
to physically alter a dying person's appearance and, after
that individual's death, to assail all those present within the
room as they sought other victims to conquer.[25] Such
personification of evil forces is *not* to be taken lightly or
dismissed out of hand. The mere presence of independent
assassins implies an inherent evilness of the sort that can
affect physical objects and corral the thoughts of well-
disciplined soldier types (those that permitted St. Peter to
escape were executed by Herod, which they undoubtedly
knew would happen if they *consciously* allowed their prisoner
to escape).

That professional assassins may not be *who* they
appear to be is simply a byproduct of his or her profession.
That they may not *act* as if human belongs to the influence of
parties best left undiscussed by the timid and weak-minded.
They are, whether conscious agents or not, foot soldiers of
Satan, primed and prepared to kill for whomever pays.

---

[22] Luke 8:30, *NAB*
[23] Ibid, 32-33.
[24] Acts 12:6-19, *NAB*
[25] See Godlewski, R.J. *Of What Price, Heaven? Encountering God Within a Highly
Secularized Society* (Charleston: CreateSpace Independent Publishing Platform,
2013), 1-5.

# A LEGION OF ONE

DEMONIC SPIRITS REMAIN a subject often ridiculed as either fantastical superstition or the realm of imaginative religious persons eager to shepherd a flock into believing a fabricated ideology. Most of these charges come from those who, although many profess scientific mannerisms, simply dismiss that which cannot be observed directly or qualified through mathematics. Nevertheless, one cannot assume that the "entire" universe is physical any more than he or she can suggest that a person's nighttime dreams always remain based upon factual firsthand experiences.[26]

The human brain may, indeed, serve more as a limiting valve rather than an organ of perpetual cerebral growth. This thought is supported by tales of drug intoxicated or mentally ill (not to mention the possessed souls in the Bible) persons achieving "superhuman" strength. We cannot possess within our limited *human* minds what exists outside the physical attributes of the universe. We cannot comprehend *pure* intellectual beings.

Understanding independent, professional assassins is equally difficult for his or her trade is one that is either caricaturized by Hollywood or dismissed by law enforcement and security practitioners. After all, there remain few if any examples brought about by the press, public authority, or personal admission. No legitimate autobiographies to cull information from or historical records to support investigative proceedings. It is almost as if the trade did not exist at all.

In our discussion, we have based our thoughts upon

---

[26] The author, for instance, experiences dreams of places never visited, speaking languages never encountered, while completing complicated mathematical equations when his conscious Calculus skills are virtually non-existent.

the concept of evil itself, most notably that of demonic spirits that possess both the bodies and thoughts of men and organizations. We could argue, truthfully, that such thoughts inspired billions upon billions of people to adhere to various religious faiths ranging from Judaism on through Christianity and, finally, Islam. A pretty remarkable feat if Evil – against which requires joining either of the foregoing – did not exist.

Perhaps the greatest evil in the world remains its ability to conceal its presence. That is, evil's greatest camouflage is to make people ignore its reality for then the enemy remains free to prowl amongst us. If we choose to blind ourselves to *any* threat, then we effectively hide it from our efforts to combat it. Deception rules in physical or spiritual combat – and in privately procured assassinations.

What cannot be deceived from the analytical mind, however, remains the extraordinary challenges that do confront the independent killer. Not the least of these challenges remains the aforementioned need to eliminate any thought of an assassination once it occurs. Could any professional athlete ignore the reality of his or her winning the championship once that goal had been obtained? Could any entertainer or musician relinquish the glory associated with winning an Oscar or Grammy award?

The only people that come close to these challenges remain, perhaps, government intelligence personnel whose work rests within compartmentalized security, but even they bear the knowledge that their minds are not the only ones containing his or her exploits. Not so with the independent contractor whose job remains to kill for a living. No "Assassins Anonymous" for him or her to seek out psychological support.

An assassin's mind – independent contractor or not – boggles the imagination of most everyone else. Despite that 65% of the human population *could* kill, it is necessarily done through acquiescence towards an authority figure. Few could do so without an *active* partner; hardly any could do so without telling *someone* – even if only within a suicide note. Killing, again, remains a deeply personal action; to kill another human being and keep it all a secret exerts a profound disturbance upon the psyche and even killing in full witness of others causes many to experience trauma and lasting repercussions. What must lurk through the mind of such a professional creature?

St. Peter offers a suggestion: "Your opponent the devil is prowling around like a roaring lion looking for [someone] to devour."[27]One could easily imagine a professional assassin prowling around as if a roaring lion but, perhaps, he or she is simply a human tool of the devil. Surely when Cain killed his brother Abel, there were no group dynamics in play; his murder was dealt with through the actions of a solitary figure, though one largely inspired by the same serpent that thrust his parents out of Paradise.

Despite the connotations of evil and its presence within private assassinations, we still must draw the line on culpability. However strong the demonic influences may be, the *assassin* bears the guilt for his or her will remains far stronger than any demonic temptation. It is only when the individual devalues it themselves does a person's will become weak enough for him or her to give it away freely. In this regard, perhaps, suicide bombers bear a stronger will in that he or she patterns their entire life around the hatred implied in blowing oneself up in order to kill an enemy.

An assassin, by contrast, working exclusively for pay bears no such recognition for they are merely equating human individuals *not* with a hated enemy, but merely as timeclocks to punch in order to receive pay. Such mechanization of lives remains unconscionable to the foundation – not even affording humanity the briefest trait of warm-blooded companions.

This is why Hollywood action movies generally focus upon either contract killers or glorified death; viewers must

---

[27] 1 Peter 5:8, *NAB*

be able to affix some level of emotion into the process in order to digest the ends. For example, whenever a villain turns out to be rather emotionless and inhumane, viewers (and critics) are likely to expound the virtues of the actor's performance as if *that* adds emotion to the character for our convenience.

The truth remains that independent contract killers exist. They *are* human, and their career focuses upon killing *other humans*. That said, evil exists within the world to specifically target humans (all the evil demons were tossed out of heaven at the same time and as pure spirits, their 'trial' period remained instantaneous compared to humanity's decades long lives). This means that independent contract assassins – no matter how brilliant and contemplative they are – are no masters for beings that do not grow tired, hungry, weak, or make mistakes.

Into his or her mind flood innumerable demons that serve little but to instigate, persuade, advise, and propel that individual to kill for a living. And to kill with cunning efficiency and cold-blooded concern. No emotions to cloud the mind; no regrets to cease the profession. To kill and then to forget. Truly, it boggles the rational mind. In Figure 2 we observed how that mind forms a competitive nature at its core, resting upon the very basis of survival. Because of this, human nature rests upon being able to brag about one's career; to challenge others within this do or die world of competitive excellence.

As previously discussed, it is likely that independent assassins never evolved out of this phase of mental development; that his or her eternal "competitive/survival phase" keeps them from disclosing *anything* he or she does – itself a seemingly diabolical trait. That they had never ventured into "alliance building/cooperation" or "society building" layers of thought support this conclusion. They are eternally fixed from considering the welfare of others.

That human evolution *did* go through this phase at one period, it is nevertheless difficult to understand precisely *when* humanity moved beyond the present assassin's mindset. Because this was obviously well before the onset of written languages – and even, perhaps, oral traditions – it is difficult to find comparisons within the historical record. Possibly, the most recent facsimiles involved the earliest renditions of Aztec and similar cultures that dispensed with people through systematic sacrifices. Yet, even first century Rome – that burned Christians alive as garden torches for the benefit of the emperor's guests – still valued *some* humans as worthy of concern. As did Nazi Germany and Soviet Russia.

Our problem, in analysis, is that we must remember we are dealing with secluded *individuals* – not segregated societies where the ruling class remains free to do whatever it wants with the underprivileged (largely through emotion-filled hatred). Pure individuals are exceedingly hard to decipher for they maintain no associations, no strong friendships to learn from or manipulate. Their only interactions with society in general remain tainted through deception and cover. Yet, they are not supermen (or women).

Sometimes, even, professional assassins blend in too well with society, leaving that proverbial "traffic jam" of disruption to an otherwise chaotic flow of humanity. As with B-level Hollywood movies, occasionally an actor acts too much, giving away his or her desire for something a bit more glamorous. For example, during egress from a crime scene – most notably if viewed from a security camera – a killer will not act sufficiently panicked, even if he or she attempts to stagger through the scene of fleeing citizens. That is, even their motions through a crowd may appear too artificial for the events surrounding them.

Furthermore, they may – depending upon the situation and timing – act too civilized when others may turn berserk. For instance, common protocol requires assassins to egress away from the crime scene via public transportation that offers view tangible observers and yet permits uncooperative witnesses. However, during some crises, many people simply flag down – or commandeer – the first available mode to escape the terror. Someone nonchalantly boarding a bus *may* seem strange to a practiced eye.

All of this, of course, depends upon the assassin functioning within expected parameters. They do not, which is why most of their victims die innocently by way of "accident". No need to run away from a crime scene if no such scene exists. No investigation required for commonplace incidents. Their actions are, again, most sinister if not openly diabolical.

Militaries the world over have been trying in vain to condition soldiers to kill with such cunning, but they have yet to emulate humanity's most "ancient enemy". It absolutely confounds the mind to consider an adversary that intimately understands 13+ *billion* years of universal history. Modern people have *no clue* as to what – and *who* – we are up against, so prevalent is our belief that we remain superior to everything except, perhaps, alleged extraterrestrials (which undoubtedly do not exist for the same reason that humanity is unlikely to survive long enough to venture into space before demons force us into a battle royale against one another).

Turning back to independent assassins they, like most entrepreneurial professions, do not diversify as much as their more bureaucratic brethren. They are not likely to engage within drug trafficking, human smuggling, or illicit financial opportunities beyond requisite money laundering. Assassins, of the type being discussed here, remain *purists*. They do one thing and do it exceedingly well. When it comes to surgical killing, they remain history's undisputed gold medal champions.

With his or her encyclopedic knowledge of specific individuals, vast repertoire of empirical techniques, and accomplished ability to disappear into the night, quite literally at times, the private assassin bears few enemies. This, perhaps paradoxically, illuminates the contract killer's demonic influences. Rarely do evil individuals lash out at one another. This can be ascertained quickly by examining the evening news on television; just observe how each major political party views the opposition. One or the other is very likely to cry foul over the opposition when its own participants engage wildly within the same vice. The same rests true with Hollywood figures who often bear the standard for hypocrisy.

In the animal kingdom where survival is of paramount importance, like-species rarely fight until death. Elk, for instance, will lock horns and battle for hours but do very little damage to one another. Contrast this with an encounter with a wolf or a coyote and either elk bull is likely to dispatch the predator with ease. The same holds true with evil individuals though some suspect the situation, say, in urban Chicago argues against the point. The Windy City's problems, unfortunately, rest with territorial survival rather than mere protection of the criminal species itself.

Assassins, by virtue of his or her trade, are likely to remain protected by any demonic spirits that condemn the rest of the planet for the obvious reason that running out of pliable individuals would prove detrimental to their efforts. Most people, it can be argued, remain relatively lazy for the benefit of abject evil. Even in temptation, we faulter and resist – but *not* for civic reasons. To engage within assassination as a productive means to disrupt humanity, any evil spirit could not count on those whose mannerisms depict sloth and inconsistency.

Perhaps this is why the Biblical Legion implied possessing individuals with countless numbers of demons. The diabolical infestation of a single, relatively weak person by numerous demonic spirits exceeds even the imagination of the wildest Hollywood screenwriter. In responding to a question from an experienced priest as to the precise numbers of demons affecting humanity, a spirit simply replied that were they visible to the human eye, they would easily black out the sun.[28] While not suggesting that this represents how many demons possessed the innocent soul in

---

[28] Amorth, *Exorcist*, 17.

question, it does suggest that humanity is vastly outnumbered by the spirits seeking our destruction.

Even a few dozen evil spirits remain extraordinarily destructive for people, each perhaps leveling a particular temptation – unceasingly – at an individual. One could only imagine how each element of an assassin's task is vetted out and micromanaged by such individual devils. Far easier to envision, say, than attributing these abilities to a range of psychological disorders for even serial killers relinquish to raw emotion when plying out his or her trade. For the contract assassin, such brutality would leave too much forensic evidence behind for the authorities. It must be emphasized, too, that serial killers proceed uninterrupted largely due to understaffed agencies rather than their ability to cycle through the public unnoticed.

Incredulity remains evil's – demonic or human – best disguise. When people imagine murder, they see gunfire and stabbings, drug gangs and sociopaths. They do not understand people falling down stairs, off of horses, or Code Blues in the hospital as necessarily murder per se. Nor could they imagine the breadth of premeditation that goes into some relatively "normal" murders, even those that remain glued to CSI-type television shows and whodunnit fiction.

However they view methodical murders, the public rarely dresses the issue down to a single human being. There are *always* accomplices, reasons for the crime, or even environmental considerations to implicate someone *else* for the transgression, brutality, and victims (the latter even blamed on occasion). Much of this, of course, remains in hindsight. Yet, the independent contract assassin does not foretell the range of psychological issues that illuminate the existence of other criminal loners.

The best example of this is, of course, the infamous Unabomber Ted Kaczynski. Although railing against technology, Kaczynski used the local and national media to print his manifesto. Despite his seclusion and aversion to company, he had to venture into society to both mail his packages and purchase his supplies. Even this "deranged madman" could not break the bonds of that which he hated enough to kill. Contract assassins simply work *within* society rather than revolt against it. He or she merely uses things – devices, situations, and, yes, people – as tools of the trade.

They have essentially *dehumanized* the civilian population so much that *anything* attributable to society becomes an inanimate object – and this remains the crux of his or her presence within our world. They can manipulate people's lives merely because he or she views them as if just another piece of furniture within one's living room or kitchen. With less concern over where an individual places, say, a new dining room set, the contract assassin will target a victim or employ another person's presence to affect a particular killing.

Such an introverted concept of the world remains indicative of the private contract assassin. Nevertheless, such blindness to human lives leaves the professional killer fully ignorant of the *true forces* aligned against him or her. Theologians attribute these forces to evil spirits – Satan and his lesser devils. From this perspective, the demons cause sin through deception, accusation, doubt, enticement, and provocation.[29] Deception and doubt, arguably, represent the worst of these attributes because they serve to shield or conceal reality.

Deception offers a chance to turn attention away from natural (e.g., the presence of demons) forces towards the artificial (e.g., sociologists' blaming crime upon various aspects of one's environment). Doubt, for its role, merely hides reality through incredulity (Devils? *Really?*). If an individual sees fellow human beings as less than human – one does not generally kill one's peers – then he or she is not likely to understand the demonic threat against such human persons. This represents the deception inherent within doubt itself; we, as a society, refuse to believe that of which we do

---

[29] Thigpen, Paul, *Manual for Spiritual Warfare* (Charlotte, NC: TAN Books, 2014), 12-14.

not *want* to believe.

Because private contract assassins are, obviously, quite rare in their talent and function, it goes to be recognized that they do not hail from a particular race, nationality, creed, or sex. Whereas hatred – as a raw human emotion – exists within *all* people to some degree, indifference remains foreign; few can go through life without affixing some measure of concern towards *some* others, regardless of how tiny that pool is. People are social creatures – even those *anti*social individuals that seek to maim and kill at whim. To remain functionally indifferent requires a complete abdication of the human condition.

If an individual does not believe within the sanctity – or any perceived value – of human life, then he or she cannot subscribe to *any* religious practice for religion itself requires a lifetime of effort to protect that sanctity. Some professionals balk at this reality, stating such nonsense as, "[w]hat a tragedy for the world that not one of the great spiritual leaders – Abraham, Moses, Jesus, Muhammad or the Buddha – was *brave enough to say that he did not believe in life after death* [emphasis added]. Is this the biggest confidence trick in human history?"[30]

Such statements as that referenced above are not only blatantly ignorant – "spiritual leaders" specifically deal with the spiritual (i.e., that involving life outside the corporeal) – they imply broad confusion generated by both deception and doubt. Only a spiritual demon could suggest that Abraham, Moses, (particularly) Jesus, and Muhammad represented confidence men, for history has proven the sincerity – if not factual truth – inherent within their beliefs. To suggest that untold billions of individuals had been duped by what one single author depicts as a scam underscores the inability of some military and security professionals to gaze beyond his or her own prejudices.

Independent contract assassins, therefore, remain

---

[30] Rooney, David., *Guerrilla: Insurgents, Patriots and Terrorists from Sun Tzu to Bin Laden* (London: Brassey's, 2004), 242.

comparatively nonjudgmental; his or her treatment of the entire human population as mere "tools" equalizes them within the eyes of indifference. Nor are they likely to dismiss the beliefs of billions throughout the past 5,000 years out of personal animosity or self-inflated superiority. Such fraudulent analysis would compromise any success within his or her mission.

Given that professional killers of the type addressed within this discussion operate fully within society and, yet, outside its concern, we must, once again, address the mannerisms for which he or she is likely to wade through that social pool without getting wet. With no support groups, confessionals, or even recognition to energize their professional progress, one *must* consider the alternatives flowing within his or her mind. Simply put, *who* is training them, guiding them, and, beyond all else, *protecting them.*

If demons are, literally, legion in scope and can blot out the sun if observed by the human eye, then they vastly outnumber the population of the earth at any given time. Similarly, if they are immortal and free from the aggravations of physical bodies, then they are forever digital – never vanquished from fatigue, injury, disinterest, or distraction. If not forced away by sacredness, there is *nothing* that will keep them from doing everything within their power to destroy human value.

Into this, some logic must be applied. The battle against demons must be asymmetrical; that is, evil spirits could not attack individuals where they exhibit strength and faith. Nor would diabolical effort be applied strongly where the victim remains within the demonic fold. A teacher inspires, for instance, whereas a jailor demands. In a similar manner, evil spirits are not likely to waste time – though some do – targeting recognized saints. It is only during the sainthood process – as many begin life as abject sinners – is the battle more pronounced. Conversely, because so many people are amiable to sin, future "saints" may receive more than his or her share of temptation because Satan is likely to attempt to catch "the big one that gets away" as all proud sportsmen can relate.

Returning to the discussion of professional contract assassins, we can observe where the demonic encapsulates the traditionally human. People bear an inherent desire for happiness, but very often seek such happiness within transitory pursuits and objects. Assassins, as people, remain little different and seek things that, perhaps, few others consider – notably pastimes and collections that foster creativity while addressing his or her clandestine and largely mobile nature.

They see their function as largely entrepreneurial, almost specifically pragmatic, and take great pride within his or her accomplishments. Yet, they do not exhibit happiness in the same manner that the rest of the world's sinners do. Happiness for the assassin rests with, again, *control*. He or she *must* control their lives in order to survive and, herein, is where they most emphatically do *not* possess control. They are, perhaps, the most singularly responsive person on the planet, but their minds, their hearts, and their souls rest influenced by a legion of diabolical thoughts, desires, and actions – all orchestrated by the unseen, the unfelt, and, for most of the human population, the unimaginable.

# FINAL SKILLS

INDEPENDENT CONTRACT ASSASSINS, by nature, elude the comprehension of even the most literate security practitioner. As with the demons that arguably guide and control them, most "rational" professionals simply dismiss their presence as fantastical or the subject of misguided interpretations of existing murderers. Nevertheless, as with the evil spirits that swirl amongst us, assassins *do exist,* and it remains a breach of the imagination to assume that they *all* work solely under the auspices of governmental or criminal organizations.

Part of this reluctance to admit existence rests with the natural inclination of the modern human mind to attach some measure of "certification" to professions. This remains the basis of the Entitlement layer expressed within Figure 2. Regardless, every profession on the planet – be it medical, military, law enforcement, etc. – began as the sole domain of independent providers. These healers, mercenaries, and armed guards only gave way to licensed and documented professionals when their numbers warranted regulation by those seeking more revenue for civic treasuries and private associations.

In contrast, due to their extremely low numbers and purpose within life, contract killers will never rise to the attention of national legislatures and local professional organizations. To assume otherwise remains an affront to societal welfare. If we cannot observe spirits that could blot out the sky, we would never worry about individuals that likely number less than a hundred within a sea of billions. Such would be like searching for an individual Mako shark that devoured a particular mackerel. The capacity is there, just not the incentive.

With thousands of murders going unsolved annually within the United States alone, suggestions of contract assassination draw the ridicule of everyone not vested in the puzzle as each professional steadfastly protects his or her own position. Sociologists, for instance, stick to accusations of environmental mishap, politicians focus upon inanimate objects, and law enforcement personnel underlying vices such as narcotics, terrorism, or immigration. Theologians and clerics, conversely, see the reason but not always its manifestation; attributing all human sinfulness to either anger, covetousness, envy, gluttony, lust, pride, or sloth.

Because emotion often manifests itself within human endeavors, people tend to blanket society's problems on his or her pet excuse. Illegal immigrants, for example, may either be neglected souls seeking a better life or mere invaders of another country depending upon one's preference for social action or the law. Similarly, taxation may be justifiable for the common good or simply a way to enslave a population depending upon where an individual stands in relation to how much he or she is gaining or losing from his or her paycheck. Emotions define perception of both legislation and evangelization (whether the latter is holy, or agenda based).

Contract assassins, of course, are *not* emotional citizens. Nor is sinning a particularly emotional function. Sometimes motorists speed, not that they are in a hurry or even wish to ignore the law, but because they simply want to motor along at another rate. It need not be emotional to remain beneficial. Or simply perceived as such. Within the workplace, many employees routinely manipulate the timeclock, punching in at the last possible moment and even milking breaks for extended periods. Emotion cannot reside as the underlying reason they remain less punctual than their more professional coworkers.

While some people speed or work with inattention, others remain indifferent to others' right to live. The abortion debate remains fluidly emotional but drops exclusively upon whether the fetus rests as an organ or a developing human life. Assassins, nevertheless, *know* that their victim remains an active human person – they just do not accord them any right to live. Here is where mere "sin" – defined colloquially as an infraction of the law – turns into diabolical behavior. People generally see murder as a means to arouse his or her anger towards whatever vice infuriates them the most. It is only when we remain ignorant of the crime – through inattention – that we emerge as emotionless.

Hollywood action movies and violent videogames remain popular because they *depict virtual representations of human actions* – not real events. The coy simply say that because these remain virtual manifestations, they are as much 'fact' as a father saying that they will kill a boy if he so much as lays a finger on the dad's daughter. Films, television shows, and videogames merely excuse us from death through their "victimless" environment (until one fails to draw the distinction between virtual and reality).

Assassins, of course, need not distinguish between the virtual and the real because he or she is not averse to acknowledging his or her function. They simply do not squander precious time on fabricating excuses for their role as a professional killer. If they pay value to *any* human being, it rests with their own survival – and that of any family that he or she may possess. Their function is to kill ruthlessly and with great skill in getting away with the murder. This implies profound de-escalation in attention and absolution of guilt through demonic influence.

Two examples underscore the precise nature of such diabolical presence – one from Biblical tradition and the other from the modern, secular record. For two thousand years, almost everyone – whether Christian or not – can tell you *who*, precisely, betrayed Jesus to the Cross: Judas Iscariot. Yet, very few can tell you *why* one of the closest individuals to God Incarnate (as an apostle, one of the twelve, Judas would have discovered Christ's divinity long before the betrayal) would have turned against his master.

In the Gospel of John, we learn that the "...devil had

already induced Judas...to hand him over."[31] Luke's recitation takes this a step further: "Then Satan entered into Judas..."[32] First Satan prepped the battlefield by, undoubtedly, working on Judas's weaknesses of doubt, perhaps, and then quite literally possessed the apostle to ensure that he carried out his new master's diabolical ambitions. When the possession left him – following Christ's death, Satan would not have needed Judas – the former apostle was left with such grief that he killed himself never expecting Jesus to forgive him.

From the modern record, we hear the tale of an Arab *teenager*, working as an assassin for the Palestinian Liberation Organization, professing his joy on television over slicing and chopping up his victims after they had been tortured for days with electrical shock, gouged out eyes, removed tongues, and castration.[33] His demonic joy obviously did not end with the dissecting of his victims, but carried over into announcing his actions for the entire world to notice. His immaturity, perhaps, could not lead to the terminal regret that Judas Iscariot suffered.

These two examples show that evil can manifest itself within anyone and within different ways. That Judas was older, and more experienced than the Palestinian teenager, undoubtedly caused his demons to attack him more cerebrally than emotionally. In essence, Judas had to have been taken over completely – body and mind – before he could betray his friend. The Arab, to the contrary, seemed to possess a video gamer's fascination with blood, gore, and acting out suspicious childhood fantasies. The common thread, again, remains diabolical influence.

In between these two extremes lays the mindset of the contract professional killer. Someone who can kill a good friend, if necessary, but without the fanfare exhibited by a

[31] John 13:2, *NAB*
[32] Luke 22:3, *NAB*
[33] Sockut, Eugene, *Secrets of Street Survival – Israeli Style* (Boulder: Paladin Press, 1995), 98.

fanatical Palestinian kid. On the one hand, he or she is required to carry out their assassination with the same apparent disconnect as did Judas Iscariot in his betrayal of an individual that did little more harm than clean out a sacred temple from greedy merchants. As with Judas, it is obvious that the assassin can carry out a most brutal – if not graphic – crime without as much as blinking an eye. Had they bore the same regret afterwards, however, they would certainly retire upon completion of the first assignment.

Considering the alternative, to kill with as much fanaticism as the young Arab, the assassin's crime would certainly draw the attention of the press, public, and all but the smallest law enforcement agency. Not to mention, the forensic evidence left from torture and mutilation would fill the coffers of police laboratories for years. Despite both examples representing satanic influence, neither would work within the career of the professional assassin as each instance acknowledged admission of the crime to varying degrees.

To kill, and to kill repeatedly, requires the assassin to view each case as a separate and *new* contract, devoid of any connection to interested parties or patterns of habit. From the strictly artistic – read that, *creative* – aspect, it remains almost inconceivable for the innovative spirit of a human being to avoid telling even friends about his or her accomplishment. Even analytical personalities, such as accountants, occasionally boast about his or her prowess at board meetings and professional seminars.

Other killers, ranging from narcotics traffickers on through legitimate soldiers during war, often brag too about their exploits, if only to diminish the psychological stresses imparted from a decidedly brutal occupation. Even shoppers engage within fisticuffs to partake of a comparatively minor sale which he or she can then boast about to other customers. To brag about success is amongst humanity's oldest sins.

Assassination, however, comes through two of the

methods of demonic preference: doubt and deception. Conspiracies, as but one example, cast doubt as to *who*, precisely, killed the victim. Government covert operations, for their role, intentionally employ surrogates and pawns to sway attention away from the sponsor's involvement. For the independent assassin, however, *both* preferences must appear for them to sneak away with the crime; deception in causing the death to appear accidental or normal and doubt as to whether a crime had, indeed, occurred.

Our discussion of private assassinations reflects upon the most sinister of human activities and, by extension, suggests the role of demonic influence. That people can kill – or wish to have others killed – is as old as humanity itself. People kill in battle, on the streets, in the homes, and, all too often – beginning perhaps with Andrew P. Kehoe in 1927 Michigan – in our schools. Individuals kill friends and acquaintances, neighbors and coworkers, family and stranger alike. They kill infants, children, and the elderly by the millions. Entire systems of government – from Nero's Rome to Hitler's Germany and Stalin's Russia – have killed more people than exist within many nations. Some of the most horrific state-sponsored crimes herald from relatively little-known cultures such as the Aztecs and Incas. If there were free will humans living upon other planets or within other galaxies they, too, would be killers. *Why?*

Because, in Christian tradition, humans represent God's loftiest creation; a species both of body and spirit. One in which God Himself chose to become part of, much to the displeasure of a great many solely-spiritual beings who chose to become demonic rather than adhere to divine plans. These beings fought to keep their pride in their superior intellect and position in Paradise intact, but they failed miserably because "Who is like God?" – Saint Michael and his fellow angels – defeated the rebels and cast them out from Heaven.

Destined to prowl the physical world until the end of time, Lucifer and his minions – a.k.a., Satan and the Fallen Angels – turned their superiority and intimate knowledge of the physical world and its laws upon the most innocent creatures ever known, Adam and his wife, Eve. From the first moments of Eve's succumbing to disobey God, her children throughout the ages carried on the precepts of sin and the consequences of forever remaining impure sinners. Her very son, Cain, became history's first murderer.

Yet, all of this – it remains argued – was within God's Plan for Salvation of the human species. His Incarnation proved to the world that even the most horrific of sins could be forgiven, if we only opened our hearts to the commandments of worshiping God above all else and loving one another as we love ourselves. Divine generosity and love opened the doors to eternal bliss for man and woman, young and old, rich and poor, slave and master, educated and uneducated, regardless of race, nationality, or status.

Thoroughly insulted over losing his princely status as, perhaps, the angelic world's most illustrious resident, Lucifer decided to rebel against God's Mercy and took as many underling spirits with him as he sought to divide and conquer the human race as best as he could. He would show God – and the good angels that battled him out of Heaven – that people were no match for his cunning, his deceitful ways, and the allure of earthly positions and passions. God may be King of the Universe, but Satan, in his mind, was lord over the earth.

From Cain's filial murder on through today's massacres in schools and houses of worship, the Devil – antiquity's "divider" – worked to keep people from coming to accept both God's infinite mercy and His desire for them to come to know *true* happiness. Instead, through diabolical persuasion, people sought temporal happiness through wealth, success, lust, and recognition. The more he or she gained, the more he or she wanted.

When others become widely more successful and "blessed", the sins of envy and jealousy cause them to morph into resentful and bitter citizens of our communities. When lawsuits and other grievances could not be affected through entitlements, many sought to even the score through crime and they stole, misappropriated, or conned the innocent. Still, others remained more successful – even more honorable in his or her dealings. For those who could not steal his or her way into success, they decided to end the presence of adversaries.

Killing became a way of achieving this fame and fortune. First the killing, in prehistoric times, became legitimate survival; ensuring that families of the "strong" possessed enough food to eat. Nevertheless, when killing became easy, it also become quick to solve. Soon murder not only kept food on the table, but interlopers away. From there, the practice became sport – and tribal responsibility. To kill became less a necessity than a rite of passage and a flag to unfurl. Entire legions of soldiers ventured off into heretofore unknown lands to kill en masse when everyone nearby chose to live through enslavement to the rich and powerful. Kill or be killed simply manifested itself from "us" versus "them" and nobody wanted to become one of *them.*

Therefore, to make killing easier for the meek and humble, people began to articulate exactly who "them" were. They were people of a different color, of a different race, of a different tribe. If you lived within a castle, they might be farmers. If you were a farmer, they might be industrialists. If you were noble, they were certainly vagabonds. If you preached elitism, then they were simply individuals seeking liberty. Throughout history, mankind continued to divide itself into atrocity.

Rome's Nero torched Christians in his garden for illumination, but the enlightened revolutionaries in France tortured Catholic priests with no less enthusiasm. Nazis in Germany tried their damnedest to exterminate Jews because they were living in Germanic lands, but Arabs conducted much the same atrocities against Jews that traveled home to the Holy Land. Conquistadors landing within the New World were considered murderers and thieves by the murdering and stealing cultures they broached upon. And every *civilized* nation on the planet has, at one time or another, ceremoniously progressed through a civil war pitting neighbors and family against one another. Bar none.

In spite of all of this mayhem and chaos, people *still* find it difficult to believe that there remain individuals professional enough to kill for a living and *not* get caught at the practice. It is as if martial brutality has become so widespread and "common" that independent entrepreneurs within the trade are out of place and an affront to accepted murder on a global scale. Perhaps it is only because he or she has dispensed with the raw emotions that justify killing on an indiscriminate scale that he or she draws the ire of many.

Killing without acknowledging the humanity of the victim seems foreign, almost "anti-demonic" in scope, but it still remains diabolical just the same and for the very reasons it instills hatred from the brutal. Apparitional horrors cannot be defended against. Ghosts in the mist cannot be confronted with. No pure human has ever devised a way of destroying a demon. Even through denying their existence, we are merely deceiving ourselves. Legislation, education, and popular entertainment cannot change the laws of nature – or *who* understands those laws better than we do.

In the modern world, people fear the drill more than the dentist, the firearm more than the thug holding it. Nowhere do we ever contemplate the rational, free willed mind behind the instrument of injury and discomfort. When death occurs, we relegate the event into a myriad of other grievances as if to say, "If we had only banned drills, then our dentists would find more patients to serve!" And so we offer up legislation to pass "anti-drill" laws and permit ourselves to go around with devastated teeth.

To simply deny that professional assassins exist – or that we can actually know about them and how they function – dismisses both the dentist and the drill in a very real sense. For without dentists, we exclaim to ourselves, there would be no pain of the drill (never minding that if we took better care of our teeth, there would be no need for either). Of course there *are* dentists within the world and a great many of them. We know they exist because we recognize them through experience, research, and, above all, their *presence* within our midst. They do not attempt to hide for to do so prevents them from gaining patients.

Assassins, on the other hand, bear a skillset no other professional hones: complete and utter secrecy. Even covert government agents spring to life for Hollywood movies and non-fiction best sellers as soon as their career ends. The only difference between them and that Arab teenager, perhaps, rests with his or her reluctance to talk about castrating individuals for pleasure or intelligence. But they do; let there be no doubt about it. Just because most people remain civilized does not negate the presence of those who do not care about personal liberties or the rule of law.

Contract assassins – as independent businesspersons – own the rules he or she follows. It guides their efforts, accepts their clients, and seals their fate (whether comfortable retirement or eventual capture and incarceration). Whatever rules they follow, they manifest their desire to kill through a most diabolical dehumanization process. When fueling both an art and a science, it remains best to leave emotion out of the equation for passion negates the scientific method and analysis sours the creative spirit. In this way, the independent assassin merely does "a job" even if few others are capable of doing it. As with a retail sales associate, they go about their role with a mixture of acquiesce and resolve; a paid professional doing a job they know well the best way they can.

A professional with a truly demonic skillset...

*Mark 16:17-18*

# ABOUT THE AUTHOR

R.J. Godlewski (pronounced GOD LESS KEY) is the former executive manager of a threat resolution services business and served as the president of his own security company. He is an alumnus of American Military University, holding an M.A. in Military Studies, Asymmetrical Warfare concentration and a B.A. in Intelligence Studies, Terrorism Studies concentration (with minor degree in Area Studies, Middle East), both earned with academic honors. He further holds graduate and undergraduate certificates in Security Management and Explosive Ordnance Disposal, respectively. Mr. Godlewski is a veteran of both the U.S. Navy and U.S. Navy Reserve. He remains devoted to protecting the dignity and integrity of innocent human life, wherever and whenever it may be placed in jeopardy and by whatever means may be necessary and employs the breadth of his knowledge, experiences, and assets to achieve this mission.

His previous books include:

*Effective Hunter-Killer Operations*

*Practical Guerrilla Warfare*

*More Skills of the Assassin: Delving Deeper into Human Depravity*

*Skills of the Assassin: Understanding the Tactics of the Professional Killer*

*Fourth-Generation Corporate Security: Asymmetrical Warfare for Protective Services Professionals*

Made in the
USA
Middletown, DE